MUSIC HAS LEGS

First Published 2020 by Good Stories Publishing, LLC.

Library of Congress Catalog Number: 2020908357
Library of Congress Cataloging-in-Publication Data
Music Has Legs.

Music Has Legs.
By: David Haznaw & Marlene Byrne
ISBN: 978-0-9777135-5-4

Based on a true story. Some of the names have been changed.

MUSIC HAS LEGS

Based on a true, triumphant story of
what ordinary people can do together.

By David Haznaw & Marlene Byrne

This book is dedicated to
Juan Manuel Pineda,
Nuestros Pequeños Hermanos
and Shriners Hospital.

We'd especially like to recognize
the staff, donors and children of
NPH,
a family that is changing the world.

Contents

Big things
often start with small beginnings.
Someone has an idea or asks a simple question.
It gets the ball rolling and gains momentum, to a
point where no one person can stop it.

Each of us has the power to say "yes."
We hope this story inspires you to be part of bigger
things that can change the world.

𝄞

FOREWORD

David Haznaw

When I met Marlene in 1991, we were both young, energetic 20-somethings looking to make our respective marks on the world.

Marlene had just founded an up-and-coming advertising firm, and she hired me as a creative and public relations director. While our time together was short lived (I left the agency after 18 months to start a business of my own and eventually, Marlene's life and career path took her to Chicago where she built her successful marketing firm), we stayed in touch, always looking for another opportunity to collaborate.

Now, three decades later, after career twists and turns, raising families and generally living our lives, I'm proud to say that Juan and his story brought us back together, once business associates, but always friends with a common goal of working on something together.

Something that mattered.

This story, of Juan Manuel Pineda, is one of tragedy, faith, friendship, opportunity, joy and rebirth. Told from three points of view, it chronicles Juan's journey from an unwanted, shamed, physically-compromised orphan living on the streets of El Salvador, to someone who—through love, compassion, boundless generosity and music—finds a path to a better life.

This story is based on real people, real situations and Juan's real journey. Characters, scenes and conversations have been developed—using some creative license—to bring the story to life. But the facts don't lie. It is, in my humble opinion, the crowning jewel of Marlene's intrepid, optimistic and sometimes fanatical work to help others, and in particular, Juan and all those involved with Nuestros Pequeños Hermanos, a network of orphanages helping—saving—children throughout Central and South America, and the Caribbean.

I've loved music all my life, as a fan and a musician. While I don't claim to be a virtuoso or expert in the craft, I believe music has powers that go far beyond entertainment. Because of that and my long-standing friendship, respect for, and faith in Marlene, I was happy and honored when she asked me to be part of this project, from the concert to the telling of his story.

As you read this book, you'll feel the sincerity and compassion exhibited by the three storytellers: Marlene Byrne, Father Ron Hicks, who is now serving as a Bishop in the Archdiocese of Chicago, and Samuel Antonio Jimenez Coreas, who grew up at NPH. These three people, along with so many others, worked tirelessly to help Juan regain his health, his sense of self, and finally, to develop his passion for writing and performing music.

This story shows that anything worthwhile involves hard work, setbacks, faith and a strong support system. I hope it has as much impact on you and your life as it did on mine.

Please enjoy and be inspired by both the story and the storytellers.

—David

♭

SAMUEL ANTONIO
I'M JUST A KID

I waited outside the building, leaning against the brick, letting the rain hit my face and chest. The sky was a deep blue with heavy clouds. Far off, over the mountains, the sun was trying to peek through. The rain felt good; better than the feeble showerhead in our backyard, and this water seemed cleaner somehow. I kept an eye on the side door, waiting for it to crack open. When it did, I started to move. I could feel my feet sinking into the mud as I ran toward the truck. The mud left spotted marks on my legs similar to the dirt splashes on the wheel flaps of the rusty, old box truck. Jorge yelled at me to get inside, but I wasn't listening. Things like water, mud and storms didn't bother me.

I ran around back and opened the truck doors wide so Jorge could load the bread. He had covered the batch with a white cloth, like a bed sheet but nicer, to protect it from the rain. The loaves were arranged on a large board, stacked in perfect rows, all stuffed in bags. I was never allowed to move the bread, and I had to be careful to stand to the side so I didn't bump him or cause an accident. In this downpour, we needed to move quickly.

The rainy season was upon us, and it always added an element of fear to the locals. Flash floods and mudslides were common in El Salvador. Without notice, an entire road could be swept away. Jorge couldn't deliver the bread if that happened, which was devastating because when you live day-to-day, hand-to-mouth, to feed our family, the bread must get delivered to get paid.

I loved everything about helping Jorge. From the smell in the truck to the sights along the road, I was always happy as we went about our deliveries. Jorge was a serious man, but I loved being with him. He was never cross with me, even when I made a mistake. I realized later that he wasn't particularly nice to me, either. But he was stable, reliable and predictable. And for someone like me, those qualities were more than enough.

I don't remember him laughing. Not once. The only time I saw him smile was when Camilla was born. I was standing in the doorway with the other three children and remember him holding her in the straight, wooden chair, next to the bed where Rosa, his wife, rested. At that moment, with Rosa sleeping next to him and the tiny baby in his arms, he was happy and content. When each new baby came, I wondered if he would ask me to leave, but he never did. I kept the other kids busy while he and Rosa tended to the baby. When I could, I'd steal a glance as they fed her, washed her and rocked her to sleep; always staying out of the way, making sure they didn't notice me watching.

I often fantasized about how Jorge felt the day he found me. It was before he started driving for the bakery; before he and Rosa had children of their own. At the time, the Sandinistas were ravaging the country. Violence and poverty were terrible so the only thing Jorge could do was spend his days rummaging through the garbage dump for food and other *tesoros*, or "treasures." It's what he called the things he and Rosa had found useful from the dump. Scavenged items, like the old foot stool and the green lamp remained in the small home, reminders of those days when survival was the main goal for Jorge and Rosa.

"Imagine my surprise," he once told me, "I was on the garbage pile and saw something move. At first I was scared, but when I brushed aside some debris, I discovered a little hand." Jorge had found me in the trash. He used to say I was his greatest garbage dump gift. Interestingly, he told me when he dug me out, I was carefully wrapped in a blue blanket, yet so filthy he hardly recognized me as a baby.

I tried to imagine Rosa's reaction when he came back from the dump holding a child. Hardly able to feed themselves at that time, was she happy? Was he happy? I never asked. In fact, I never ask a question when I'm afraid of the answer. Jorge didn't like to talk too much about it anyway. He saw nostalgia as a waste of time. "Hard work and prayer are what's important," he would say. Jorge had worked hard to get—and keep—this delivery job for the bakery.

We loaded the truck, jumped into the seats and drove away. I remember looking over at Jorge, wondering how he could see the road through the heavy streaks left by the worn-out windshield wipers. Muddy patterns crossed the glass and changed with each swipe. The sound is still clear in my mind; a scratch going one way and a thump on the swipe back. He rarely spoke while we drove, and this made the "scratch-thump" of the wipers seem to grow faster and louder with every mile.

After our third stop, we turned toward a mart located on the outskirts of town. I ran to the back of the building to hold the doors open for Jorge. At seven years old, doors were really the only thing I could do to help. Jorge would carry in the bread and collect the money, like always, and then we would leave.

This place had gas, groceries and a long rack of candy. Even though I was never allowed to have any, I loved to look at the colorful candy packages and read the labels. One was caramel, another had nuts. And then there were the colorful sugar candies, including some that looked like worms. I always wondered why anyone would choose to buy worms to eat.

When we got back to the truck, the rain had stopped. That was common here. It would rain hard for bit and then stop, making way for the humidity to set in. We were headed back to town with one stop to go. Coming over a hill, we saw a car parked in the road, blocking our path. I wondered if there was water in the roadway. Or maybe it was an accident. Or maybe the car had gotten stuck in a rut and couldn't get out.

Before I could see what was happening, Jorge yelled at me to get down. I didn't move. "Down on the floor!" he yelled again. It was a tone I had never heard from him. He wasn't mad, he was panicking. I was frozen and couldn't take my eyes off the two men who were quickly approaching the truck, one on either side.

The man on my side was looking right into my eyes. His face was unshaven, and his shirt was dirty. His eyes darted from me, then down the road, then to his friend and back again. The other man suddenly pulled the driver's door open. He had a gun and was yelling at Jorge to give him our money. Without a word, Jorge started to rummage between the seats, among various papers and notes he had made for himself. He grabbed a green zippered case and pulled out a few bills. Then, there was an argument about how much money he should have. I had never seen this zippered case before and realized it was a decoy; not where Jorge kept the "real" money. The argument continued and the man on my side yelled, "We have to go."

I heard a loud crack. It was a sound I didn't recognize. Then, another. This one made my ear hurt. The man on my side had already started running away, back to their little car. The second followed and he had the case. I looked at Jorge and saw blood on his arm. My head ached from the noise. The pain was so fierce, I put my hand behind my ear. When I drew it down, my fingers were full of blood. I didn't know what to do, so I just sat there, staring at the road.

The men sped away, and time seemed to stand still. I don't remember Jorge starting to drive or any part of the journey to the hospital. I was frozen in the seat. I have no recollection of Jorge's injuries or how he was able to navigate through traffic, but I remember him repeating, "It will be okay, it will be okay, it will be okay," over and over. The next thing I remember is my car door opening. It was chaos when we arrived at the hospital; everyone coming to the truck, taking me out one door and Jorge out the other.

I would never see him again.

♪
MARLENE MARY
I'M JUST A SMALL TOWN GIRL

I grew up in Brillion Wisconsin, a town of 2,500 primarily white, terminally middle-class families. My parents both worked typical Midwestern jobs, Dad as a patternmaker at the town's largest employer, Brillion Ironworks, and Mom at a local bank.

I'm the youngest of three. Colleen was shy but played the role of the responsible oldest child to a T. Next came Dick, confident and outgoing, completely breaking the mold of the "forgotten middle child." Then there was me, always moving, always curious, always impatient; following closely—often too closely—behind both of them.

My childhood was simple and frankly, a lot of fun. In Brillion, everyone knew the Farrell family, but that's not unusual because everyone knew everyone. We were Irish, Catholic and lived in small-town America, which I saw as the trifecta. Our neighborhood was like something from a Norman Rockwell painting: kids always outside playing and riding bikes, parents sitting on porches, barbequing or doing yard work.

Most days, our biggest problems were broken shoelaces or trying to explain to our folks the reason we didn't do well on our social studies test.

And of course, when you're living in classic Middle America—replete with Saturday night trips to the Dairy Queen and Friday night high school football games—you have a family pet, which in our case, was Penny.

Penny was a mixed-breed (or as Dad called her, a mutt), with crooked ears and a tail to match. I remember Dad bringing her in the house on a Saturday afternoon. He yelled for us to come downstairs and there she was, skinny and skittish, her fur thin and matted. She was hiding behind Dad's leg as we all tried to get in close. "Where did you get her?" Colleen asked. "She just appeared in the back seat of the car," he answered. Dad would never tell us the real story. Every time we asked him, the story would change: a stranger on the side of the road handed her over, or she just showed up in a basket on the front porch. To this day, I still don't know the real story, but it appeared to me—to all of us—that Dad had saved Penny from a life of neglect.

Over the first few weeks, Penny got stronger, filling out to a healthy weight, thanks to a regular feeding schedule (something I'm sure she didn't have in her previous life), and the occasional table scraps we'd give her despite Mom's rebukes whenever something "accidentally" left the table. This led to Penny becoming something of a beggar when food was around.

We all loved Penny. She was social and good with people. And she had come along at the perfect time in my life. My siblings were teenagers and at an age where they were spending less time at home and more with friends, which often left me—at age 12—as the only one in the house. Luckily, Penny was always ready to play, or to go for a walk, or just to sit at my feet when I did my homework or talked on the phone with my best friend, Lisa.

When we sat down to dinner, Penny's nose would rest on my lap as if to say, "Hey Mar, don't forget about me!" And I never did.

Penny and I had a bond. When I left for school, she followed me to the door. "Take me with you!" When I came home, she greeted me with a wagging tail and a wet nose. "I knew you'd come back!" At night, she snuggled in while I watched TV, always the companion, especially on nights when I was home alone.

This was true the weekend the carnival came to town. The trucks had rolled in Monday and the workers spent all week setting up the colorful rides and booths full of prizes, blocking the streets of town and creating anticipation for the weekend. Once a summer, the carnival would come to Brillion and all the kids would run from rides to games and back again, feeling a sense of independence as their parents hunkered down in a tent with neighbors.

My friends and I loved the carnival. We purchased a bundle of ride tickets and moved from the Scrambler to the Tilt-A-Whirl to the Ferris wheel. In between, we used food tickets to get cotton candy, popcorn and anything else we could get our hands on.

I remember my parents walking me home that Saturday night. It was only a few blocks from Main Street to our house, but they promised to get me in the house and settled before they walked back to the music tent. My mom especially didn't like me at the festival at night because she thought it was too wild. I wasn't sure what that meant, but she seemed concerned about it.

I locked the door behind them and decided to camp out on the living room floor with a sleeping bag, popcorn and candy collected from my day. I would enjoy a quiet night of watching whatever I wanted on our only television as I rarely got to control the station. I sat close to our console TV, a piece of furniture that took up a corner of the room, changing the channel with the silver dial until I found the show I wanted. Penny, curled up next to me on the sleeping bag, was out cold, snoring.

She never moved until she heard strange voices outside. A group of people was walking past, laughing and talking. Penny growled. I sat up straight. I heard firecrackers in the distance. We never had any action on our street. When I turned the volume down, I could hear the music, and it seemed like all the noises and voices were close; too close.

Penny started barking, and I didn't stop her because I thought her bark might scare whoever was outside. Together, we checked the locks on all the doors. It felt like someone was out there watching so I went around the house and closed any gaps in the drapes. I decided to go upstairs to look out the window from a dark room. Up and down, the street seemed empty. Back downstairs, I remember turning the volume back up, and within minutes, my parents were home.

I couldn't remember a time when I was ever really alone in the house because Penny was at my side.

One day, I walked in the house and she wasn't there to greet me. "Odd," I thought, as I called her name. In the kitchen, Dad was sitting at the table, home from work early. He looked up at me without his usual smile, and I immediately knew something was wrong.

"I'm so sorry Mar."

I looked around. "Where's Penny?"

"She's…gone."

Time seemed to stand still as I stood there frozen in the middle of the room. In an instance, everything drained out of me. She was gone. My friend, my Penny. Dad stood up and put his arms around me, holding me tight like only a dad can. It felt good, and I wanted to let my feelings out but I didn't.

"How?" I asked after a moment.

Dad hesitated, and took a deep, long inhale. I could feel his lungs expanding on my cheek.

"She ran out into the street…" I didn't hear anything after that. I didn't need to. I didn't want to.

I broke away from him and ran up to my bedroom. I needed to be alone. It was there, on my bed, in the comfort and safety of my room, my refuge, that the emotions started to flow.

I cried every tear in my body. The tears released and there was no way to stop them.

I would never see Penny again.

\#

&

RON
I'M JUST A CITY KID WITH A BIKE

I remember everything about that bike. My parents bought it as a gift for my 12th birthday. In the morning, my dad rolled it into the kitchen as I ate breakfast. It had a huge bow on it, just like how these scenes play out in TV commercials and movies. But that morning, there was no time to give it a test ride, because we had a party to prepare for.

Mine.

That afternoon, friends, neighbors and relatives all gathered at our house in my honor. It was great, and under usual circumstances, I would relish the attention, soaking in every card, gift, compliment and accolade. But on that sunny summer day in 1979, all I could think about was getting rid of these people, so I could get on that beautiful new Schwinn Sting-Ray.

For months, I'd been begging for the bike with its classic bucket saddle seat and sparkly paint job, and my parents had delivered. It was perfect, Campus Green (the official Schwinn color) with "chopper-style" handlebars and a 3-speed stick-shift on the crossbar.

My friends were in awe when I showed it to them. Before the party, we had wheeled it out to the garage, still boasting the oversized bow, to put it on display for all to see. They all begged for a chance to ride it, but Mom told them I should be the first as she guided them to the cake, a distraction no sane pre-teen boy could resist.

We played games while my new pride and joy sat in the garage, leaning on its kickstand, like the coolest kid in school leaning against the wall in his leather jacket, a toothpick dangling from his lips.

Finally, after the last guests had left, I was free to ride it, and ride it I did, as fast as I could, the wind cooling my skin and blowing back my hair. As I pedaled, I made up my mind that Matt was the only one I would ever let ride this bike. Matt was my best friend, and I knew I could trust him. The other guys might try to jump curbs or let it fall when they got off it, but not Matt. They might give me a hard time for shutting them out, but I decided to be honest and say I didn't trust them with my newest, most-prized possession.

Besides, Matt was the biggest kid in our class, and if he told them to stop teasing me, they'd listen. That's the kind of influence he had. Unlike the rest of us, Matt never had to prove he was tough because everyone just assumed by his size that he was not to be challenged. I knew he'd never hurt a fly, and so did Matt; but we both loved the fact that no one else did.

I turned the corner as the sun started to set. The bike was perfect, easy to steer and pedal. It felt like I was flying. I remember turning the corner and starting down the hill by the Schultz house. They had five girls all named with the letter J—Jean, June, Joan, Jane and Jill. The girls were some of my favorite neighbors and I was hoping they would be outside to see me ride past.

First pedaling and then coasting, I picked up speed. I stood up and leaned forward into the handlebars, trying to go a little faster. The blocks were long in our neighborhood and the houses set back, with big front lawns and short fences. They seemed to fly by as the Sting-Ray rocketed down the street.

Out of nowhere, I felt a hard thump, and without warning, I lost control. Next thing I knew, I was on the ground. It's funny how you don't really remember the fall, just the shock after landing. My handlebars had turned sharply into my side. I hadn't seen the uneven sidewalk. It came up so fast. Now, on the pavement, I stared down at drips of blood as they hit the concrete. Time seemed to stand still. I think the shock momentarily paralyzed me as the blood ran down my leg. It was also dripping off my elbow. I realized I needed to move, and I tried to pick up my bike. It was mangled. First walking and then running as best I could, I left the bike, headed for home and burst in the door yelling for my mom.

In my bed that night, I remember her sitting by my side. I had bandages on my forehead, arms and legs, and she was comforting me. She had given me my choice of candy from the basket above the refrigerator and had let me go to bed without making me brush my teeth.

"Don't worry about the bike, Ronny. We'll get it all fixed," my dad called from the door. He had gone back to retrieve it after my fall.

I never saw that green bike again.

It must have been damaged so badly it couldn't be repaired. Dad replaced it with a new one, a red one. I never told any of my friends, not even Matt, why the color changed. No one ever asked.

Since then, I've never liked the color green.

$\&$

CHAPTER ONE

FATHER RON HICKS
WALKING IN THEIR SHOES

Upon my arrival at NPH El Salvador, I was escorted to the office of the home's director, Olegario Campos. As I sat down and waited quietly, I recognized the smell. It was the same combination of cement, cleaning solution and children that had become so familiar to me while I was in Mexico. It was clear that my time there, with Father Wasson, had influenced me and ultimately, brought me here to El Salvador.

Olegario's office was sparse by American standards. It had a metal desk, two unmatched metal guest chairs and a filing cabinet. There were folders everywhere, neatly stacked in high piles on his desk, on the other chair, along the wall, and ironically, on top of the filing cabinet. I assumed they were case files of the children, both those residing at the orphanage and others looking for permanent homes with the help of local social workers.

A Crucifix hung on the wall to my left. Behind the desk was a large portrait of Jesus, hung next to a smaller photograph of Father Wasson.

Father William Wasson was the founder of Nuestros Pequeños Hermanos (NPH), a group of orphanages established in 1954. At that time, he was serving at a church in the Tepetates market district of Cuernavaca, Mexico called "The Church of the Poor." One morning, the sacristan came running down the aisle to meet him, explaining that a thief had robbed the church's poor box the night before. In Mexico, nothing was worse than a "church thief."

That afternoon, the sacristan again came to Father Wasson with news that the thief had been apprehended and was in custody. Father Wasson would need to go to the jail, make a statement and complete some necessary paperwork.

Upon entering the police station, Father asked if he could meet the thief. To his surprise, it was a 15-year-old boy who explained to Father that he had stolen the money because he had no family and no money for food. Unwilling to press charges, Father Wasson appeared before the judge on the boys' behalf, stating that the boy could live with him at the church rectory for the next four years while he attended school. This boy became the first *pequeño* of NPH.

The judge was impressed with the priest and his willingness to not only forgive but rehabilitate someone who had wronged him and his parish. He contacted Father Wasson and sent eight more orphaned boys to his church the next week. It would be the beginning of the NPH home in Mexico.

Father Wasson had that effect on people. They followed him like he was a shepherd, not because he asked but because of his solemn resolve and sincere compassion for others. He was the most steadfast, focused and driven person I had ever met. Yet he was gentle. Gentle with each and every child who came to NPH. Gentle with his staff while commanding the utmost respect and demanding hard work. Gentle with volunteers like me, who came to NPH to give something back to humanity.

I had volunteered at NPH Mexico for a year in 1989, working directly with the children. Even today, I vividly remember so many details about that time. It changed me; so much so that when I returned to the States, I knew two things.

First, I knew I needed to change gears and do something with my life, something that had meaning.

Second, I knew I would always be part of the NPH family and

someday, somehow, I would return.

I had to.

So, when I left Mexico and returned to the States that fall, I announced to my family I was entering the seminary.

The experience with Father Wasson was an important factor in calling me to the priesthood. During my discernment, I struggled with the idea of not having a family of my own; never marrying and sharing life with someone, instead giving my life to God.

But five years later, I made good on the promise to myself. I was ordained and assigned to work as a parish priest in and around Chicago, which I did for the next 11 years. Now, it was time to return to the people and the place where it had all started. Francis Cardinal George had given me the opportunity to leave the diocese and work for Father Wasson as the NPH Regional Director for the homes in Central America, including El Salvador.

I was startled when Olegario entered his office. He moved quickly, carrying a mound of papers that he set down on the side of his desk as he settled in. He cleared a few things away and then leaned back in his chair to look at me.

"So, Padre, please tell me, why do you want to be here?" he asked.

As simple as it was, the question caught me completely off guard. The funny thing is, I had been asking myself that question—or at least a form of it—all my life: "What am I doing here?" In other words, what was my "Why?"

For a moment, an uncomfortably long moment, I just sat there, staring straight ahead, past Olegario, looking directly into the eyes of Jesus. He seemed to be looking at both of us. In the portrait, he was not on the cross, but in a beautiful setting, happy and smiling. His eyes were soft and friendly, and they spoke to me. I responded, "I have to be here."

"You... *have* to be here?" Olegario was trying to understand what I was saying.

"Yes. It's... my home in a way. It's my calling; the right thing. I knew years ago, when I worked with Father Wasson in Mexico. And now is the right time."

I guess that was the answer he was looking for because 20 minutes later, Olegario was showing me to my quarters, telling me dinner would be served at 5:30 p.m. sharp, and to let him know if there was anything—anything at all—I needed.

"¡*Bienvenido*!" he said as he shook my hand.

"*Gracias*," I responded, and as I closed the door, the first thing I noticed were the green walls.

Ugh.

Before I even looked around the room, all I could think was, "I hate green."

I took a deep breath, the kind you take at the beginning of an adventure, a big test, or just before you dive into deep water. Then, I started to unpack, neatly folding and organizing my shirts. Even as child, I was neat. I liked my things in their place, including my food, never allowing one item to touch another on my plate. My parents were always accepting of me and my quirky ways. I loved that about them and hoped I had inherited their ability to appreciate children for who they were and to see things as opportunities rather than problems.

I believe those formative traits stay with you throughout your life. I used my experience to carry humility into my vocation as a Catholic priest, and it always seemed to connect me with those I met at NPH and later, with the parishioners I served.

I believe—and will always believe—as a priest, I must walk in the shoes of those I am sent to help. Every time I think about this philosophy, I remember a specific phys. ed. class from my childhood when I had forgotten my gym shoes, and the teacher—a stereotypically gruff, plainspoken wrestling coach—threw a pair at me from the lost and found. He simply said, "Wear these." It took me 10 minutes just to get the first shoe on my foot. (All I could think of was all the germs that had taken up residence in these old, stinky shoes.) Sick to my stomach, I was finally able to lace up both shoes and make it through the class. It reminded me that walking in other's shoes could be both uncomfortable and difficult. But sometimes, it was necessary.

Now, walking in the shoes of others meant something much more; to "Let go and let God" help me understand "the shoes" of others. And I became good at it. I'd sit and eat with the locals, on the dirt, without washing my hands. I'd go days without showering, and often, my clothes weren't neatly folded and stowed as they had been every day of my previous life. It was hard, but it was necessary, and overcoming my old habits and quirks was more than worthwhile.

Beyond the dirt and dust that came along with traveling to a place like rural El Salvador, I had to get used to the sheer simplicity of life and how hard these good people had to work just to survive in an area plagued by such blatant poverty. I'm an educated man with an undergraduate degree in philosophy, a Master of Divinity and a Doctorate in Ministry. Except for my time at NPH in Mexico, I've lived in highly-developed, first-world cities all my life. But I loved the work and had made a promise to this dusty, poverty-stricken outpost in Central America.

Father Wasson had asked me to accept a long-term position as the organization's regional director, a five-year commitment. It was then it hit me, as I sat down on my "new" old bed, in my new green room, in my new home. I'd be here for the next five years.

The position required supervision over orphanages in El Salvador, Guatemala, Honduras and Nicaragua, with El Salvador serving as my home base. But more to the point, El Salvador would give me a purpose and a place to walk in the shoes of the real people—children, families, workers—living in poverty.

𝄞

CHAPTER TWO

SAMUEL
I'M HOME

To say I hated it there didn't begin to describe what it was like. Dirty. Disgusting. Smells I couldn't identify. They called it an orphanage, but if you saw it, the first word that would come to your mind would be "prison." And believe me, that's what it felt like to be locked up in that place. The block walls. The chipping paint. The empty hallways that echoed every sound. It was eerie. Depressing. It wasn't home, but for now, it was *my* home.

I was just a kid, sent to this place because I had nowhere to go, no one in my life, and nothing except my name. And after three months I even hated that, thanks to the bullies that constantly taunted me, beat me and berated me, using my name as a weapon against me.

After Jorge died, I moved in with his brother, Julio, and his family. Even though life there was sometimes difficult, it was paradise compared to this place. I can't tell you exactly how many months I had spent at this orphanage, but I will tell you on the day I left, I was bigger, tougher, wiser, and if it's even possible for a 10-year-old, more cynical than when I arrived. But even with all that, the day the bus pulled up outside the gate to take us somewhere else—a "better" orphanage—all I could think was that my tragic life was changing again. Déjà vu in the worst possible way.

I was part of a group of kids assigned for transfer to a new orphanage, called Nuestros Pequeños Hermanos. No one told us why or asked if we wanted to go. As much as I hated where I was, the last thing I wanted was to move and start over again, reliving the same horrors I had endured here.

We woke up to a knock on our doors and someone telling us to pack our few belongings and meet in the yard where we would be given instructions. "Bring everything," they said, "because you're not coming back." Bittersweet, but mostly bitter. That's how we were treated back then.

Arriving in the main courtyard tired, confused and hungry, we were told what was happening and given a small sack of food to eat along the way. Minutes later, there I was, sitting on a small bus, being taken away from one hell hole only to be dropped into another.

I had taken a seat in the back, like always, feeling like I needed to keep everyone in front of me, where I could see them and any trouble that might stir. We were told nothing about this new place, but even though I hated where I had been living, at least it was familiar. The bad food, the constant bullying, the occasional abuse by staff when we didn't do our chores on time or to their liking.

My life had been a series of terrible circumstances, which seemed to get worse with each new "adventure." Because of that, I always prepared myself for tragedy and heartbreak. The bus started along the bumpy road to the next phase of my life. I could hardly stomach the anxiety.

What was around the next corner?

As the trip progressed, I watched my young life flash before my eyes. With every mile, I was reminded of where I had been. I thought about my mother and father, people I never knew, but I fanaticized how life might have been different if they had kept me. I remembered Jorge, his stoic countenance, absence of emotion, wondering always if he loved me, but never doubting that he cared. I recalled the wonderful smell of his bread truck, and helping him make deliveries. And the shooting. Oh my God, it seemed like a lifetime ago, yet the fear, hatred and deep sadness were as fresh as the day it happened.

Passing through a village, I saw a man shouting at a young boy, pulling him by the arm. It made me think of Julio, Jorge's brother, the man who I had hoped would save me and give me a new and better life after Jorge passed. Unfortunately, Julio didn't see me as the son or the nephew he never had. I was just an indentured servant to him, property he used and abused for his own gain and pleasure. Alonzo, Jorge and Julio's father, had tried to save me from the abuse, but that's what landed me at the first orphanage. And it proved to be so much worse than Julio's house.

What I wouldn't give to be back there again.

Hours passed, and I sat silently gazing out the window at everything and nothing at all. All of us sat quietly. There was nothing to talk about. At times, my focus was clear, my senses on high alert. Other times, I'd check out as the miles clicked off, the sun moving from East to West.

At some point, I noticed more traffic around the bus. I sat up wondering if we were getting close to our destination. Then I saw it, the sign on the road read "Santa Ana." Could we be back near Julio's house? I tried to remember the streets and wondered if given the chance, could I make my way back there? Maybe if I found Alonzo, he would take me in. Was he alive? Maybe if I talked to Julio about working harder, he would take me back, and this time, he'd treat me better. I was a year older and stronger. I could be more help to him.

We passed through town and I sat up tall, looking for familiar things. Was that the store I used to walk through, just looking at all the items but without money to buy anything? Is that the street we walked down? It all looked familiar, but at the same time, I couldn't place exactly how I recognized it. I stared backwards as we left town, hoping to see something, anything I could recognize.

Maybe even Julio.

Once we were out of town, I sat back. "Was it really that bad at Julio's house?" I thought to myself. I started to imagine it wasn't. Eventually, I closed my eyes and fell asleep.

The afternoon sunlight woke me, but it was the smell—*that* smell—that opened my eyes.

It was a garbage dump, but around here, that meant it was also home to many who couldn't find a better option. This is a land where poverty is everywhere, and many are forced to rummage through garbage dumps for sustenance. Jorge found me in a garbage dump, just like the place I saw out the window. It was massive, with trash as high and far as the eye could see. But in places like this, it's not the garbage that draws one's attention. It's the people rummaging through the dump for food and treasure; from the youngest children (some of whom are born there) to grandparents and great-grandparents.

At 10, I was already numb to it all. And today was just another page in the book. Where were they taking me? What would happen there?

I was hungry. The lunch we had been given to eat on the bus was long gone, my stomach was growling, and I was hot.

It's always hot in El Salvador, but today's heat was affecting me more than usual. The others, some talkative and annoying, had quieted down as the hours passed. Some slept. Others, like myself, simply stared out the window, watching the scenery change and wondering how our collective lives would change in the coming days, months and years.

I was half-sitting, half-lying on the seat, hoping to fall back asleep. This time, it wasn't the smell that jolted me, it was the bumpy dirt road and the grinding of brakes. I looked out to see we were approaching a large gate, a fence with barbed wire and a high brick wall. Above the gate read, "Nuestros Pequeños Hermanos." It means "our little brothers and sisters."

We had arrived.

At first, it looked like a jail, but as the gate opened slowly, it revealed a beautiful, tree-lined courtyard with a paved path leading up to a big building.

Now we were all awake, sitting upright, our eyes wide, no one saying a word, just taking in our new surroundings. Slowly, the bus pulled through the gate and up the path. This was not like the place I had left hours ago, at least not on the surface.

Smiling children ran and played in the courtyard, waving to us, *los hermanos nuevos.* The bus stopped and the children gathered around it, eager to meet us. As the door swung open and we slowly emerged into the late afternoon heat, the group of children parted and an adult—a *padre*—approached. He was a *gringo,* clean and well-groomed, the only thing distinguishing him as a priest was his collar. Otherwise, just another gringo. (I had seen them before, and rarely did they ever help me.)

I'd find out later his name was Father Ron. But at that moment, I wasn't sure what to make of him, this place or what was in store for me, a scene that looked too good to be true for a boy who didn't even know what "too good to be true" meant. I remember looking back at the gate, devising a way to get out.

My plan? To run away the first chance I got.

#

&

CHAPTER THREE

FATHER RON
NO SHOES

The car bounced on the dirt road. I'll never get used to the dust, the dirt, the filth. The heat made it impossible to close the car windows, no matter what the filthy air did to my allergies, my lungs and even my clothes. I loosened my collar for relief and looked over at my driver Luis. Road noise deflected any opportunity—or obligation—to make small talk. It's like one of my seminary teachers said, "There is a time to observe the environment around you, take it in, and commit to it." I guess this was one of those times, but at the moment, all I could think was how much I missed air conditioning.

Luis wasn't much for talking anyway. He preferred to concentrate on the road, and that was comforting to me because frankly, by my standards, what we were traveling on did not classify as a road. But to say his silence and focus calmed me would be a lie. El Salvadorans drive aggressively, with gusto. You'll rarely see a Salvadoran leaning back in their seat and "cruising." They're almost always bent forward with two hands tightly gripping the wheel, as though driving is a competition; something to be won.

The dusty air was filled with the abrasive racket of car horns, the rumble and rattle of eroded mufflers providing the bass and percussion. What separated Luis was that he didn't yell at other drivers.

Maybe it was his personality, or the fact that his job was to drive me—a *padre*—wherever I needed to go. I wondered what he was like when I wasn't in the car. Did his driving persona change when he wasn't in the presence of a priest?

Back then, I liked to observe the difference in people's reactions and behavior when I wore my collar versus when I dressed in street clothes. It didn't matter where I was. Even my family acted more reserved when I wore the collar. It's not as obvious now, years later, but it's still there. In Central America, the respect was even more prevalent, and reverent.

As we drove, I leaned my head back, felt the breeze—hot but better than nothing—closed my eyes, and knowing I wouldn't be able to sleep or even relax, opted for prayer:

Dear God,
Give me strength for what I am about to see.
Keep your strength in my chest, close to my heart.
For with you, I can stand tall and strong.
Bring your gentle touch to those I serve.
And please bring a cool breeze.
Amen.

The car jerked to a stop (the NPH "limo" was in desperate need of a new transmission), and immediately, jarringly, my eyes popped open. We were here, though at that point, I wasn't exactly sure where "here" was. I had been asked to make a visit by one of our staff members. They knew of a family that was in dire trouble but would not give me any details. This happened a lot, like talking about it was more embarrassing for them than simply sending me here to see for myself. All they would say was that I should meet the family and administer to the sick mother, pleading with me to pay them a visit next time I came to town.

Luis knew the neighborhood, and I assumed he probably knew the whole story, but I didn't ask. He pulled up to a house and cocked his head to the side, indicating which one I should enter.

Always a man of few words.

I stepped onto a small stone slab in front of a simple doorway. At the edge of the small front yard devoid of grass, sat a small house set back from the street. You might have missed it altogether if you didn't look. I had been to many homes like this, simple and small, with dirt and stone yards where we as Americans would expect to see green grass. Yet so many times, these homes were filled with more joy—and people—than the large homes we're accustomed to in the U.S.

"*¿Hola?*" I said into the doorway, half asking if anyone was home, half announcing my presence.

Nothing. I looked around the property. There were other houses up the street, but it was quiet everywhere, save for a small dog running through the yards. I turned back to Luis still sitting in the driver's seat and shrugged. I knew he would be no help.

Luis never left the car during our visits to the community. At first, I thought it was because he didn't want to see people suffering, especially his people. Later, I came to realize it was because he didn't want the *banditos* to steal the car. After all, a driver without a car is simply unemployed. And as the driver for NPH, Luis spent his days running supplies and driving the teachers in from Santa Ana. He resisted driving for me; he thought there were more important missions, but Olegario forced him. In time, I would need to find another solution for my transportation needs.

"*¿Hola?*" I again inquired, this time louder and with more authority. I stepped with one foot into the open doorway and looked into the small front room.

A head peered around the corner, low to the ground, a small boy with a severe cleft palate. Like so many of the children here, it had never been fixed. He said nothing.

"*Hola, me llamo Padre Ron.*"

The boy moved toward me, slowly and awkwardly. At first, I thought he was sitting on the floor. As he moved around the doorway, he pressed his knuckles into the ground and thrust his torso forward. I realized that he didn't have legs; just stubs that barely extended past his hips. The bottom of his shorts swept the dirty floor and a puff of dust rose each time he moved forward. He stopped and looked down.

I realized I had stepped back, like I was planning to leave, but it was simply a reaction, a reflex upon seeing a child in this condition. Even with all the things I had seen, this caught me by surprise. I couldn't help but look directly at his legless body and contorted face. I couldn't tell if he had stopped because he was following my eyes or if he had noticed my recoil and was looking down in shame. His eyes remained fixed on the floor.

I took a slow, silent breath and stepped toward him. I always tried to meet those I reached out to eye-to-eye. So, I sat down, cross-legged, on the dusty floor directly in front of him, close to him, probably closer than he wanted. Now, it was his turn to be surprised. He moved back slightly.

"I am Padre Ron," I began.

Slowly, he looked up. He had beautiful brown eyes and high cheekbones. The closeness of our faces helped me focus more deeply on him as a person and not his abnormalities.

I waited. He didn't say anything. I wondered what he was thinking about me. Up close, I saw him as more beautiful than from afar, but maybe I had the opposite effect on him. Did our proximity make me less likable? Then I thought, "Maybe he can't speak."

Seconds passed, and the silence grew deafening. It took all my energy to just sit there and not fill the gaps with uncomfortable small talk. After a moment, my patience paid off.

"*Me llamo Juan Manuel*," he said quietly, almost a whisper, as he looked me up and down. I guess I deserved the scrutiny.

I spoke in Spanish. "Juan Manual. How old are you?"

"Nine."

I reached out to shake his hand. He was dirty. His shirt was small and stretched tight across his torso. I noticed his muscles. His chest and arms bulged unlike most boys his age.

He looked down at his hands. I knew he was embarrassed by the dirt they collected "walking" on them. He wiped them on his dirty shirt, and slowly reached out to my open hand. I grabbed it firmly, sincerely, and used my second hand to grab his arm as well.

"I am here because Anita wanted me to visit Maria. Is she your mother?" I asked.

"Yes. She is in back." His head cocked slightly to indicate the location of the room Maria occupied. His eyes remained fixed on me. Then, after a long pause, he continued. "She is very sick."

"Please let her know I am here," I replied, "and see if she is able to talk with me."

Juan turned and swung his body quickly through the doorway. I was amazed at how nimble he was. As I stood up, I noticed the heat had made me sweat through my clothes, the dust clinging to me, staining me, but also bringing me closer to these people. I wanted to pat down my pants, but I stopped. If Juan returned, he might be embarrassed by my actions, almost like I was wiping away our conversation, regretting ever coming to this place. As much as I tried. I would never get used to the dust and dirt that came from the dry climate. It was only better than during rainy season when everything turned to mud.

In my previous life, I always prided myself on cleanliness, and it took all my effort not to remove the dust from my pants. I needed a distraction, so I looked around the room.

The home was plain like so many here. By American standards, it seemed empty. A small table with a lamp and two chairs sat in the corner. A softer chair with a small footstool in front of it was under one of the two windows. A Crucifix hung on the wall in the famous Llort style. (Fernando Llort Choussy was a Salvadoran artist, often dubbed "El Salvador's National Artist," and this Crucifix was a replica of his design style, which could be seen all over El Salvador.) The colors brought a childlike happiness to the room.

Moments later, Juan appeared in the doorway. I decided the best thing to do was smile. It's amazing what a universal symbol it can be.

"She says you can come." I followed him through the doorway.

Maria was lying on a mattress on the floor. There were

pillows, a flat sheet, stuffed animals and a family photo around her. A water cup, tissues and a book were neatly arranged on a short, three-legged table beside her. It was obvious she was being cared for and deeply loved. Her body was thin, but she wore a clean dress, her hair combed with a braid coming down her shoulder. I'd imagined how beautiful she had been prior to her illness.

I walked to her bedside as Juan pulled a chair across the floor to me. She smiled and tried to sit up, but I could see she was pain. Juan moved back to give us room.

"Juan Manuel, go outside while I talk with *Padre*," she said.

Juan went to the door and hesitated. "¡*Sal de aquí*" she yelled, and I was startled by the strength in her voice as he disappeared.

Immediately, Maria grabbed my hand and again, her strength surprised me.

"How are you feeling?" I asked.

"It doesn't matter," she replied as she waved her other hand. "*Padre*, I know my time is coming."

"Shall we pray together?" I asked. The opportunity of talking with God together is such a powerful way to generate a relationship, and it's something I never underestimate.

"I mean no disrespect," she said quietly, "but please do not pray for me. The Lord does not see us. We are too lowly." Then, she repeated the previous sentence, this time quieter. "He does not see us." Her tone was matter-of-fact, with a flat effect that belied the statement she had just made.

"God sees everyone, perhaps more often the poor and sick and those in need," I replied.

She looked down and rubbed the back of my hand. "I know you believe it, *Padre*. I can see you are a good man. But I believe he doesn't see us. We are invisible. I am not mad at him for it. I just know it to be true."

"Maria, I don't understand why bad things happen to good people, but I believe God is always with us." I truly believed what I was saying, yet I knew I was not going to change her mind. And I didn't blame her for feeling this way.

"Then why? Why was my boy born with a mangled face? Why did a fire take his legs? Why did my husband—his son's father— abandon us when we needed him the most? And now, as the only one to care for him, I am dying." She locked her eyes on mine. Her gaze cut right through me, making me uncomfortable. Yet I knew I shouldn't—I couldn't—look away, not if I wanted to earn any respect and credibility with her.

I tried to talk, but she held up her hand, and I realized that there were some arguments best left alone. She needed me to be silent and just hear her out, so I decided to simply listen.

"Look at this life. Do you see your God here? If He is here, I don't want to know him. This place, this pain, this is not the God I know."

Her voice became hoarse, and she grabbed the half-filled glass of water next to her bed. "What do I say?" I asked myself, trying to slow down my thoughts. I wanted to give solace without being too forward or strong, but I knew her burden was heavy. I decided I needed to know more. I took a deep breath before I spoke.

"How did the fire start?"

"I don't know. No one does. We were selling in the market-place, my husband and I. Juan's older sister was supposed to watch him. She was 10 years old. But she left him as he slept. When the fire started, she was outside, and they didn't find Juan until a beam had fallen across his legs."

Her head bowed, and the loose hair from her braid fell over her face. She shook her head from side to side, unable to finish. I leaned forward and touched her knee through the sheet. "But Juan survived, and he seems fine."

"Fine? You think a boy with no legs, a mangled face and no parents will be fine?" she said. "After the fire, his father left before we even returned from the hospital. So, if you want to pray, do not pray for me. Pray for you." She was looking right at me.

"For me?"

"Yes. Pray that you have the strength to live up to your God and your words. Because you will be tested. And you will need all your faith to help Juan."

I didn't know what she meant. My face gave away my confusion as she grabbed my hand.

"I mean no disrespect, *Padre*. I can't believe in God, but I can believe in you. I know God sees you. He hears you. And now, all I care about is to see that you care about Juan. I want you to take him, to bring him to your orphanage and make sure he has a life. Then, I can die in peace."

I sat up straight. I knew I couldn't take in a child without involving social services, paperwork and approval from the leaders at the home. Even as I talked with her, I knew that the government of El Salvador was working to take children out of the orphanages and place them back with their relatives. I hated my next move, but I had to divert her question and gain some ground without making a promise that I might not be able to keep.

"Maria, I think Juan Manuel will want to stay right here with you. What if you recover? What if the doctors can help you?"

"I won't recover. My days are numbered." Her resolve was clear.

Thirty minutes later, I left Maria. My hand was sore from her grip. She had held it tight the entire visit. Even with her persistence, all I could promise was to look out for Juan Manuel and try to secure placement for him. I could talk with social services, but I didn't have any real power with either the government placement services or the admissions director at the NPH orphanage.

During the rest of my visit in the city, I felt like Maria's hand was still squeezing mine. I kept shaking it out, but I couldn't get rid of the feeling. Had she broken a bone? I was distracted as remnants of our conversation kept popping into my head.

We finished our errands, and by the time we started our return trip to NPH and the familiar landmarks dotting the roadside, I began to feel better. The ride back brought a sense of relief. Again, I prayed.

Dear God,
Please put your hand on Maria.
Give her comfort from the pain
and release her of worry.
Guide me in helping her transition to you.
And lead me in helping Juan find a place in this world.
Amen.

I opened my eyes. Praying in the car relaxed me, and in fact, made me forget about the bumps and potholes in the road. Today, my prayers seemed empty, so I stared out the window.

We passed by the huge, mountainous garbage dump where trucks unloaded trash from a road at the top. It was easier to pass by this place now, since the government had moved the "shack village" away from the bottom of the mound. I always hated seeing families working the piles of trash, digging in the garbage for anything they could find as sustenance. Today, it was devoid of human life. Where had they gone? Were they surviving without the garbage dump village? What if moving them out of the dump worsened their plight? I certainly felt a sense of relief because I didn't have to see them, but I wondered if they were any better off.

We turned down a dirt road and saw the families who lived just outside the NPH gates. They had brick homes with dirt floors and clotheslines, fires for cooking and boiling water, and chickens in their yards. The children, dressed in T-shirts and shorts, always smiled and waved at us. They were some of the happiest faces here. As we passed, Luis gave them five short beeps on the horn, uncharacteristic for his stoic personality, but it was a ritual he performed with the kids whenever he passed. Sometimes, like today, it took all my energy to wave back, but I always did. We were the only people they saw, and I often wondered if they wished they could enter NPH or if they were happier having their own homes on the outside, even if it was a simple existence.

In the distance, I saw our gate. "Welcome to Nuestros Pequeños Hermanos" was carved into a wooden sign hanging over the entrance. You would think an orphanage—with its high fence and barbed wire—would feel like a jail, but it didn't. I laughed because the fence kept the *banditos* out, preventing them from stealing our food and supplies as much as it kept our children in and safe. Funny how restrictions can go both ways.

As the gate opened, the car pounded familiarly on the pavement. We were home. The grounds of NPH were not indicative of the world we came from. There was grass. There were brick buildings with glass windows, all intact. A flagpole stood in front of the school at the center of our circle drive, and on it flew the flag of El Salvador, with its three stripes, two blue and one white, an intricate coat of arms located in the center.

To the left, on a hill, sat my house. Olegario had moved me out of my green dorm room and into my own quarters on campus, away from the children. After the day I had, all I wanted to do was get there and shut the door behind me. But much like the country kids outside the walls of this place, the NPH kids always greeted me when our car returned, making a quick exit impossible. Their huge smiles and happy faces told the story of their life and family here at NPH. Again, I prayed a silent prayer:

Dear God,
Thank you for this place.
Keep my spirit strong as I continue your work.
For here are the little ones that matter.
Bring your gentle touch not only to them but to all those I serve.
Oh, and please bring a cool breeze.
Amen.

Luis swung the car to the front of the school, and I saw the children racing over from the soccer field. Thank goodness their favorite sport required only a ball. As I got out, Luis drove away to park the car behind the school, where it would be safe. He worried about the kids touching his car and drove away as soon as he dropped me off.

"¡*Hola!* What are you doing today? How about some homework?"

"This is our homework," replied one of the girls on the grass. "We are practicing our dances for the show."

Dance and music were a big part of the children's lives. I loved to hear them sing and dance. Their energy made my Sunday masses come alive. When you preached to a congregation of 476 children, you had to use a few tricks to get them interested and keep them engaged.

"What show is this?" I inquired. I knew they were preparing for a musical show in school, but I loved to hear them tell me about it. They were all talking at once.

"We are dancing the *Xuc*," a small girl responded.

"We are singing," said another.

"I have to dance with a boy." The others laughed at that comment.

I always kept moving as I talked to the kids in the yard. If I didn't, I caused a virtual traffic jam and never got anything done. So, I kept walking slowly as they all gathered around me and talked, some walking next to me, some following behind, others walking backwards as they told stories of their day.

In the distance, I saw Olegario, approaching quickly, walking with purpose. He always walked with purpose. Since my arrival, we had developed a respectful, easy relationship. I wondered if it would be tested when I told him Juan's story.

#

CHAPTER FOUR

MARLENE
IT'S A FIESTA

I remember standing in front of the closet, the clothes hanging neatly in a row, organized shortest on the left, long stuff on the right. Shirts. Then pants. Then skirts and jackets. Then dresses. I put the shirts in order by color to make choosing an outfit easier. As I stood there, it all seemed so stupid. When had I decided this mattered? These are questions you ask when life gets out of control. And it makes you wonder if there was ever any control in the first place.

After everything—the hospital, the funeral, all the people and the tears—my thoughts were a blur. I moved like a robot. I don't even remember who was there, who I talked to. Who shook my hand or hugged me. I wasn't sure what day it was. I didn't know what to do next.

I took off my black dress and was about to hang it in the closet, next to my other dresses when I decided, "No, not this one. I've worn this one for the last time." I rolled it into a ball and threw it in the garbage. I think it was the first real feeling I'd experienced in months. Was it anger? Sadness? Exhaustion? I honestly didn't know, but one thing I did know was that I felt something about that stupid dress, and I never wanted to see it again, much less wear it. It was a relief, since I hadn't felt much of anything for a while.

I changed into sweats and heard the footsteps on the stairs. Little footsteps.

Matt was three and Maggie was 18 months. They didn't understand what had happened. All they knew was I was home. They bounded into my bedroom, with all their energy and happiness. When had she started walking so fast? I don't think I noticed until that moment. Maggie immediately scooted to my closet and grabbed a shoe. She sat on the floor and put her little foot inside. Why are little girls so fascinated with high heels?

I bent down to kiss her head and immediately, the odor hit me. It was time for a diaper change. What some people consider an undesirable, if not awful chore, was a parental task that made me happy. Finally, something normal, routine and regular. And it gave me a reason to get out of the bedroom. A diaper change.

Those little chores are what saved me. I didn't have time to feel sorry for myself or blame anyone for what had happened. I didn't have time to worry about my recovery. Being needed was my salvation. It's what got me out of bed in the morning, the routine of everyday tasks. Two young children will do that to you. Matt and Maggie saved both of us, Brian and me. Day by day, we got back to focusing on them, enjoying their antics, and acclimating to normal life. Every night, Matt would climb on Brian's lap for another rendition of *The Cat in the Hat*. Neither of us needed to look at the book because we had it memorized. As the boys read, Maggie danced to her favorite, *Barney*, her soft little curls bouncing every which way. I often wondered how someone without other children handled this kind of loss. I am not sure I could have.

Someone once said that if you put a group of people in a room and had everyone throw their problems on a pile, you would look closely and take back your own. I knew I was not the only one who had ever lost a child. Our third child, Christopher, died from complications just three months after he was born.

I knew others had worse problems than mine. I also knew if one more person told me, "You'll be fine," I'd lose my mind.

Smells and sounds. Do they become more pronounced when

you're introspective? If not, then why do they bring back such vivid memories? Like a great song that reminds you of a moment at a concert or makes you suddenly see your mom singing while she cooks dinner. I remember listening to Steve Winwood's *"Roll With It"* one time while cleaning my first apartment. I was so happy to have a place of my own. Today, every time I hear that song it still reminds me of that simple happiness.

The smell of grape jelly also makes me feel good because it's the smell I associate with the first steps to regaining my happiness. Opening the jar and preparing school lunches for the kids became the start of every day when Matt and Maggie began attending St. Mary's grammar school, Matt in first grade and Maggie in kindergarten.

The days had turned to months and then years. We were back to normal, and their excitement about going to school was contagious. Matt was packing and unpacking his school supplies on a daily basis. He knew other boys from preschool and kept reminding Maggie that he was going to school all day with his friends.

I had been back to working full time for a while. The ad agency was thriving, and we were busier than usual. We had just pitched a large state account, and I was knee-deep in the creative campaign for a new television commercial and website. I was really happy with the creative ideas and felt like our campaign was going to drive the program forward.

Planning for campaign execution is my favorite part of the job. I love organizing the elements with all the different agency departments. Working with the media department to define where the ads will run. Working with finance to create budget parameters. Managing production of the final materials as they roll out to the marketplace.

Growing up, my family had always valued hard work. Both my parents worked, and we worked as kids. From paper routes to the Dairy Queen, we all had jobs. And coming from a small town, we had other "jobs" as well. In the spring, everyone helped the local farm families. I always hated spring rock picking. Over the winter in cold climates like Wisconsin, the frozen ground drives up stones and rocks of all sizes, and if they aren't removed in early spring, they inhibit planting.

My dad grew up farming and said it was good for us to learn how hard farmers work. Rock picking was a simple, manual process in which an individual or small group—walking behind a tractor pulling a flatbed—picks or digs up rocks out of the soft, damp spring soil and throws them into the trailer. Small towns are like that. People help each other and never think twice about it.

Don't get me wrong, our family wasn't driven by service like some other families we knew. We didn't travel to disaster sites for the Red Cross, and none of us had run off to join the Peace Corps, but my parents believed in helping others. My mother was always driving an elderly person to church or visiting a sick friend or parishioner. I remember my father saying, "You don't go through life with two catcher's mitts on." When I was young, I never understood that. Like so many things, it was just something Dad said.

I'm not sure if it was the right time to ask me, or if "the ask" made me do the right thing. But it came, and my life would never be the same. I was dropping the kids at school, like I did every morning. Brian was working the early shift, so he did afternoon pickup. The principal stood in the parking lot, greeting the children. When she saw my car, she walked over.

"Do you have a minute to chat?" she asked as she passed me while I watched the kids enter the school.

My first thought was, "What did Matt do?" He had just started full-time, and sometimes, his high-spirited nature came out in inappropriate ways. But it was nothing like that. The parish was hosting a group from an orphanage called Nuestros Pequeños Hermanos (NPH), and she wanted me to help organize a fundraiser fiesta dinner and dance performance given by the visiting children. Up to that point, I had done nothing at school. No room mom. No auction leader. Not even lunch monitor. I just hadn't had the inclination to volunteer or get involved with the other moms. But for some reason, on this day, I said yes.

Who knows why we do what we do? Is it timing? Fate? Maybe

an act of God? I don't know, but that day, I surprised myself.

The meetings were fascinating. A woman named Katherine spent the first meeting presenting information about the NPH homes, showing us faces of the beautiful children. Those images are still imprinted on my brain. Nothing will make you feel more selfish than realizing what others face compared to you. We have no concept of need, only want.

I began learning about places I'd never even imagined. For the first time in a long time, I had purpose beyond family and work. My interest in the organization was profound. I read everything. NPH was founded when a priest in Mexico, Father William Wasson, rescued a fifteen-year-old boy who had been thrown in jail for breaking into the church and stealing the money out of the "poor" box. Father convinced the judge to let him bring the boy to his parish. Soon, the judge sent eight more children to Father Wasson, and the first NPH orphanage was up and running.

Since that humble and brave beginning, Father Wasson opened homes in nine countries, including El Salvador, which at the time housed 476 children. Babies had been brought in by social services or dropped off anonymously.

It was common for people to hand over kids—often groups of siblings—because they could no longer care for them. For these people, simple things like food, clean water and clothing were scarce or unattainable.

NPH was different than most orphanages. They took in siblings, and instead of searching for adoptive or foster parents, the organization raised the children in a loving, inclusive environment. With a focus on education and family love, the NPH orphanages were unique.

Working in advertising makes you understand the art of storytelling. Even after everything I had read and heard, I was skeptical. Was NPH sugar-coating its message? Could an orphanage effectively care for, educate and raise so many children? I was curious, and even a bit fearful, to meet the children for myself. It seemed too good to be true.

When you think about that many children, the task seems overwhelming. But big thinkers like Father Wasson don't see a half-empty glass. If you look at the most successful inventors, scientists or creators, they see beyond what normal people can envision. It's what makes them highly successful, masters of their craft. They see possibilities where others can only focus on roadblocks.

As I sat in a planning meeting, working on the details of the fiesta, I realized the conversation of the group had turned toward the barriers—the roadblocks—instead of the possibilities.

"What if the visiting children misbehaved?"

"How will we communicate if we don't speak Spanish, and they don't speak English?"

"What will they eat?"

"What if one of the kids gets sick while they're staying at my house?"

"Have they been tested or immunized for diseases?"

These are the kinds of roadblocks "normal" people see. That evening, I thought all the questions seemed practical and justified. I even asked one of them myself.

In our meetings, Katherine smiled and patiently answered all of the questions. She had heard them all before and knew once the kids arrived, the atmosphere—and our attitudes—would change.

Maybe it's because we live in a world of lawsuits or we work so hard to build lives to protect our families that we ask questions we later realize were unnecessary or even silly. We become educated about a topic and the knowledge helps us achieve a higher understanding.

Not long after I became involved in NPH, my attitude changed. That's what putting yourself out there always does. It can be learning to paint or taking a trip somewhere you've never been. It happens when we are scared or uncomfortable, not sure if we should move forward. When we get out of our comfort zone, we always learn something. Often, it makes us more open, more tolerant and more appreciative of the life we have.

Our job as the fiesta committee was to plan the fundraising

event at our parish and to find host families for the children from the NPH El Salvador dance troupe. The kids would give a series of performances in and around Chicago, but our parish had been selected as their home base. The committee had to assign the children; two per house for four nights. We also had to organize a community dinner with decorations, publicity and servers. And everything was to be donated. As Catholics, an event like this was right in our wheelhouse.

Brian and I talked about being a host family. We decided to talk to the kids about what would happen and brought it up at dinner one evening. Matt and Maggie, ages six and five at the time, were old enough to be curious. Interestingly, they asked some of the same questions I had heard from the adults at our committee meeting.

"Who were they?"

"Why were they coming here?"

"Could they speak English?"

"Why don't they have parents?"

After fielding some of their questions and avoiding several others, the kids were onboard. Matt wanted to host boys, and of course, Maggie requested girls. I never told them I was in charge of the home assignments. "We will have to see who they assign to us," was all I said.

As it turned out, many of the families preferred to host girls. I'm not sure why; maybe some people just thought the amount of energy two boys would bring to a home might be overwhelming.

As the days passed and the group's arrival grew closer, I became edgy and nervous. I kept opening my folder with the photos of the kids in the dance troupe. Katherine had provided a file of information about the children. They were all so beautiful; happy and smiling. I couldn't seem to wrap my head around them being orphaned or abandoned by their families. I wondered what conditions would compel you to give up your children. How bad would it need to be?

The day our visitors arrived, I was standing in the school parking lot with a clipboard. All I needed was a ball cap and a whistle, and you could have mistaken me for a camp counselor in a Disney movie. On my clipboard, I had a list matching each volunteer family with a pair of kids.

If you ask me, there is nothing like a well-prepared list and clipboard to make one feel organized. I knew I had everything ready for the event, but I kept referring back to the list, focusing on two names, Boris and Javier, the two boys that would be staying at our house.

I chose them because Boris was the youngest in the group, and I hoped it would be more fun for Matthew to have someone closer in age. When we made the decision, I was excited and brimming with confidence. But now, as I stood there, the person in charge, I was scared to death.

I kept a smile on my face as the other host families arrived.

\#

♪

CHAPTER FIVE

FATHER RON
OPEN UP

"**H**e is asshole." That statement, as simple and crass as it was, was music to my ears. It was the breakthrough I had hoped and prayed for; the product of weeks of one-sided conversations and long, painful periods of sitting quietly. Waiting, hoping Sammy would say something. Anything. The problem was, his timing couldn't have been worse.

Sammy had shown up at NPH two months prior on a bus with a bunch of other 10- and 11-year-olds, transplants from another orphanage. In reality, they were more like refugees allowed to escape "less-than-acceptable" situations. I had heard stories from a social worker about their previous orphanage and others like it; the dirty, rundown conditions, strict, abusive staff, severe punishments that often did not fit the crime, the kids often subjected to hard, manual labor.

As was the case each time children arrived at NPH, I was there to greet our new family members as they got off the bus. I would watch each child take their first step into this place, awestruck by the surroundings and the atmosphere. I was never sure if they were suspicious or accepting of the change. The grounds, green and spacious, smelled of freshly-cut grass. And the people. They were friendly, the children happy, smiling and freshly-bathed.

One of my favorite homecomings was a very young girl. As Anita, the social worker, and I walked her to the girl's dorm, she stopped dead in her tracks, looked up and asked, "Am I going to live in a mansion?" She had never seen such a large building.

Not all the welcome experiences were so happy. Every child had a different look on his or her face, but I smiled at each one. Sometimes they smiled back, their big eyes lighting up at each new sight, their ears perking up to the sounds of laughter from the children running and playing on the grounds, and their heads slowly turning to take in all that was happening around them.

But the children on this bus, all boys, seemed much more frightened. I noticed the last boy. He was slow to come down the stairs. Like the others, he looked and listened, but I could tell that he saw and heard things with greater suspicion.

I greeted him with a friendly and sincere (or so I thought), "*Hola. Me llamo Padre Ron. Bienvenido a Nuestros Pequeños Hermanos.*" He was stone cold. I assumed he'd experienced things the others hadn't, and that's saying something when you're an orphan growing up in Central America.

He said nothing as he passed me, ignoring my extended hand. Ignoring me. Ignoring the entire place. He looked back at the gate.

I listened for his name as our admissions director took roll call. In my time at NPH, I had met kids like Sammy. I kept my eyes on him, considering my next steps. Perhaps if we just gave him space, he'd come around.

I decided to be silent but present. That was my mantra every morning when I'd see him sitting at breakfast, alone on a bench in the cafeteria. There were mountains of activity all around him, yet he looked down at his food and moved slowly as he ate. I kept thinking, "Silent and present, Ron. He'll come around; just be patient."

I'd keep positive thoughts every day, when I'd see him at

morning mass, a non-participant; his eyes vacant and disengaged as he stared straight ahead.

And I'd give myself mental pep talks about making progress when I'd invite him to my office for the periodic "check-ins," informal sessions I'd have with all the kids to find out what was on their minds, to answer questions or just to talk.

For weeks, I'd smile at him, talk *at* him for 30 minutes or so, and then he would quietly stand up and leave. I'd encouraged the other children, those I knew as leaders, to get him involved. But nothing. Not a word. Not even a raised eyebrow. It was like he was dead inside. I have to admit, of all the poverty I had witnessed, the families I had met and all the kids I worked with who had been abused and neglected, I had never met anyone like Sammy. His face was beautiful, and I imagined how it would light up the room—the world—if he smiled.

In my frustration, I had contacted Anita to find out more about his story. She had given me a thin file folder with a few papers about his life. As an infant, a man who was not his father had brought him into a hospital. In the margin of one page, a notation read, "Man discovered baby abandoned in a trash dump." But there was no history, so his birth certificate had been "defined" by the doctors who saw him. That meant they had chosen his date of birth by guessing.

The next paper described a family death—apparently the man who found him—followed by an account of seven-year-old Sam being shot during a robbery. A case report noted that he had been removed from an extended relative's home soon after due to abuse. There were also notes about other orphanages, Sam running away from one of them and living on the streets. All the documents only cemented what I had already suspected about his terrible childhood.

When I was growing up, I saw the movie *Blackboard Jungle*, a story of a teacher trying to make a difference in a hardscrabble, inner-city school. In it, Glenn Ford refuses to give up on his students even though they disrespect him and at one point, beat him up in an alley. In the end, he's able to break through, getting to the students' ringleader (Sidney Poitier), convincing the kids they are worth something, and to use education as their springboard to a better life. I knew for every child we cared for, their success depended on their self-worth.

After waiting for weeks, I felt like that Glenn Ford character. And like him, I refused to give up. I decided I would not allow Sammy to remain numb and disengaged. I promised myself I would get through to him.

After all, it wasn't Sammy's fault, just like it wasn't the students' fault in the movie. He never signed up for the hand he'd been dealt. In fact, I often reflected how lucky I was to have good parents and a solid community as I was growing up. None of us get to choose our parents or the circumstances we are born into. It was Sam's circumstances that had forced his back into a corner, isolated from others.

I looked at Sammy differently as he sat on a small wooden chair in my office. I was sitting next to him in front of my desk, trying to look relaxed and maybe a bit "cool," hoping it would make him more comfortable. Like most days, Sammy just looked down at the floor, rubbing his hands together in his lap, eventually leaning forward with his elbows on his knees.

I kept looking at the clock, wondering at times if it was broken because the hands were moving so slowly. The deafening silence in the room, however, assured me the clock was fully operational, as each move of the second hand landed like a hammer strike. Even for me, someone accustomed to silent prayer and meditation, this type of quiet was unnerving. At 30 minutes, I stood up and walked to the door to end our meeting.

"He is asshole."

He said it without emotion or conviction, without looking up. Without even moving his elbows from his knees. He was simply stating a fact. I turned around and asked him to repeat it because it startled me. I thought our session was over and wasn't sure I had heard him correctly the first time.

"Excuse me?" I almost whispered, my hand on the doorknob.

I looked at the clock. It was 2:29 p.m. I was scheduled for a meeting at 2:30, an important one that I shouldn't miss. But this decision was easy. No matter how important the other meeting, or who was involved, I needed to stay with Sammy. Because by saying those three words, what Sammy was really saying was, "I'm ready to talk."

I quietly shut the door and returned to the chair I had occupied for the last 29 minutes. And for the last few weeks. The place where I had been waiting, patiently on the outside, but dying on the inside. Just hoping for something, anything from Sammy. And I knew what I said—or didn't say—in the next few minutes could be the "make or break" for this kid, and could determine the progress we would make from this day forward.

"Silent and present, Ron." I repeated to myself.

I took it slowly.

"Who?" I asked, speaking in Spanish, almost whispering the word. "Your father? Your grandfather? Someone at the last orphanage?"

Sammy looked at me. Another breakthrough.

"El niño sin piernas." (The kid with no legs.)

"Juan?" I'm not sure why I phrased it as a question, since there was no one else at the orphanage without legs.

"Sí."

Sammy talked. About Juan, and how *"el niño sin piernas"* bullied everyone in the dorm. I was sure it dredged up all the memories of men who had let him down or hurt him in his life. It was a turning point for Sammy, and for us.

In most cases, I would have counseled him to get along with Juan, give him the standard line, "At NPH, we treat everyone with respect and as a family." But for this meeting, I just let him vent. I was sure that Juan wasn't the sole cause of his anxiety, but if venting about one person helped relieve the pressure-cooker he'd been living in, I wanted to let him. It helped me understand him for the first time.

Ironically, it also helped me understand Juan.

#

&

CHAPTER SIX

SAM
FIRST LOVE

I was standing under a tree as I watched the bus pull out of the gate. I had a sinking feeling in my gut. I would miss Eva. No more secret looks or smiles from across the room. No more sneaking up behind her as she walked across the courtyard. We had become friends in the past few months, and I wanted to talk to her before she left. But now I had no one to tell my exciting news.

Friends. Who was I kidding? From the first time I talked to her that day at lunch, I wanted her to be *mi novia*, my girlfriend. But I also knew getting to that point would take time, and I was willing to do whatever it took to become more than just a friend to her.

Eva was a year younger, and until recently, I hadn't ever noticed her. But that's the way girls are. They're just like anyone else, and then suddenly, they change; the way they walk, talk, look and act. And in Eva's case, it seemed like that change came all at once. One day, she was just another kid—boy or girl, it didn't matter—and the next, she was a beautiful woman, with dark eyes that seemed to look right through me when we passed in the hallway.

I first noticed her in the dining hall. Eva worked in the "baby house" and cared for the little ones during mealtime. The children would be lined up on a cafeteria-style table, and Eva and the others would deliver their food and watch over them as they ate. Sometimes there was spilled milk or tears, but mostly, the little kids were happy.

This day, one of the older boys, maybe seven or eight, was walking back to his table past the babies. He was chubby, didn't run hard during soccer games, never tied his shoes, tripped on things and because of this, he was picked on. On top of that, he had a temper, which made the teasing worse.

As he rounded the corner from the kitchen, he tripped, causing his tray to fly forward and dump his food on the ground. Immediately, the other kids started laughing and making fun of him. Food and milk were everywhere, but no one went to help him. No one wanted to be the one who helped the "strange kid." No one but Eva. She walked right up to him and started to help him clean up. He immediately yelled at her, "I can do it, leave me alone!" as if it was her fault. She didn't get mad, but instead helped him up, put both hands on his shoulders and whispered something in his ear. I don't know what she said, but it calmed him down and together they finished clearing the mess. The incident was over as quickly as it had begun.

From that moment, I started watching Eva. One morning, I smiled at her and she nodded and smiled back. The next day, I said hello. Again, she just nodded and smiled. "Patience and hard work," I kept telling myself. And every day that week, when I'd pass by her, I'd say hello. And every time, she would simply nod and smile back at me.

Then one day, as I was standing in line for lunch, I heard a voice behind me, "*Hola Sammy.*" Though she had never spoken to me, I knew right away it was Eva. Trying not to show my true feelings, I slowly looked up, and as calmly as I could, returned her greeting. "*Hola, Eva.*" She was with two friends, and they both giggled. But not Eva. She just looked straight at me with those beautiful, dark eyes and smiled. As they walked away, Eva's friends continued to giggle, and just before they turned the corner, Eva looked back and waved. My heart was pounding out of my chest.

As the weeks passed, Eva and I found ourselves together, getting to know one another, talking, laughing, and even giving each other little gifts. In the years since Jorge passed, I hadn't felt a bond with anyone like I did with Eva, and it wasn't just a boy/girl thing. She was truly a friend, someone who cared about me, listened to me, and eventually, wanted me to know about her.

When I first got here, all I wanted to do was leave. And on several occasions, I did sneak out the front gate, each time thinking I was going to start a new life on my own. Each time I came back, and I'm still not sure why.

Now, all I wanted to do was stay at NPH, at least as long as Eva was here. She was the first girl or woman who had ever meant anything to me. The first one who ever cared about me. The first who might actually love me someday.

And that's what made it so important—and also so difficult—to be patient, to not push her. I needed to be different from the other boys. And I was. Unlike the others, I didn't brag or boast. I didn't show off in front of the girls, or try to act older than I was.

Over and over again, Father Ron's words ran through my mind: "No matter what, Sammy, always treat others—and yourself—with respect." I didn't always succeed with the boys, but when it came to girls—and especially Eva—I was committed to being respectful. I remembered how Jorge had cared for Rosa.

So, after months of getting to know one another, Eva and I were facing our first challenge. She was leaving the orphanage for three weeks with a group of NPH musicians and dancers to perform *fiestas* in the United States.

The night before, I wanted to tell her my feelings. But once again, I needed to be patient. Otoniel, the Director of the NPH music program, had announced that we all had to say our goodbyes to the troupe at dinner because that evening, they would be busy with final rehearsal and getting up very early the next day to get on buses for the airport. They would simply have no time for long goodbyes.

I waited for her outside the cafeteria. We both worked the dinner cleanup shift. I had a gift for her, but I didn't want the others snooping around. It would be my last chance to see her before her evening practice. Three weeks seemed like forever.

Finally, the kitchen door swung open. It was Eva, and she was alone. She smiled when she saw me, and we talked for a moment: about work, the fiestas and going to a strange country.

"I hope you have a great trip to the U.S.," I told her. She mentioned how nervous she was about the airplane ride and being away.

After a few moments, I decided it was time. "I...I have a...a gift for you." The words came out choppy and nervous as I held the gift in my fist. It was a small bracelet I had woven out of colored string.

"I hope the trip will be everything you hope for," I said. "You will meet wonderful people, I know it." I held out the bracelet. "I want you to have this." She held it in her hands but didn't look up at me.

"Thank you, Sammy," she replied quietly. "I love it. I will keep it with me always." Was she embarrassed?

We walked to her dormitory in silence. I was worried she didn't like it, or me for that matter. And when we got to her door, she quickly turned, kissed me on the cheek and told me, *"Te extrañare"* (I will miss you). Then, she was gone. As I walked away, I could hear girls giggling. I think her friends had been watching us from their window, but I didn't bother to look back. It didn't matter. I was so happy, happier than I had been since I could remember.

When it got dark, I snuck out of the dorm, hid by a tree and watched the music troupe practice in the pavilion. I realized what a commitment it was to represent NPH in the U.S. Even Otoniel, usually very calm, was yelling at everyone. People were making mistakes on things they had learned long ago. The musicians were off, the dancers stepped on each other's toes, and the whole troupe couldn't stop talking. Juan was the drummer and one of the few who seemed calm.

I heard Otoniel say, "Why can't you all be like Juan? He is on-tempo and remembering the music."

I didn't like the way Eva smiled at him during rehearsal. I suppose everyone looked up to him because he was such a good drummer. He didn't seem to get nervous. I had to agree that he was playing well, even though I didn't like him.

I confessed to myself that I felt guilty for not liking him. Juan got picked on by the other kids. As much as Father Ron and the rest of the NPH staff tried to create a loving, family atmosphere, we were all still kids. And when it's a bunch of kids who have experienced things you wouldn't wish on your worst enemy, sometimes things got personal. I mean, at some point, most of us had been fighting for our lives, so love and harmony weren't part of a "normal day" before NPH.

When you're like Juan, whose injuries were so obvious, you were bound to be teased. And when it happens, you have a decision to make. You can sit and take it, or you can fight back.

Juan often chose to fight back, but not with fists. He used words. And he was good at it, cutting right through others with those words. Most of the time, I put up with people giving him favors even though I knew the truth. He had an edge, an attitude, but we all had that. It was burned into us from our pasts, but that was to be expected given the situations we had all endured. But Juan turned all of that bitterness and attitude—along with his intellect—into an ability and a desire to manipulate situations and people.

I saw through it all; him using pity to get attention and gain privilege. After all, the children in this music and dance troupe had all earned their way in, through good behavior, performance in school and things like that. But Juan? He just showed up one day out of nowhere. They gave him a set of drumsticks and told him he was in.

It wasn't fair. I'll admit, he'd had a rough life, but we all had. And just because his injuries were on the outside, obvious to everyone, it didn't mean people should hand things to him or give him what he wanted because he flashed a smile or gave them the "poor me" routine.

I had seen Juan do it in classes or with the leaders. One day, we were about to take a test in school and he wasn't prepared. He came into the classroom with his legs on—which he rarely did—and the next thing you know his leg was falling off. He told the teacher he was in pain and needed to see the nurse. She didn't question him; she just let him go. Later that day, when I walked into our dorm, he was playing guitar on his bed. He seemed fine.

When the troupe reset, I watched every move Eva made. I noticed Juan looking at her. I knew that look. Any dislike I had for

Juan magnified. Now he was paying attention to the girl I liked, and I knew he was scheming. I wondered if she would fall for his act like everyone else.

"What are you doing here?" I felt a hand on my shoulder. I jumped. "You're supposed to be in your room, aren't you?"

Father Ron knew the answer, and before I had a chance to respond, he continued. "I'll walk with you back to the dorm, and we can talk."

Anyone but Father Ron would have punished me for being out of the dorm at that hour. Instead, he said he had been looking for me, and when he came to my room and I wasn't there, he figured I'd snuck out to watch the troupe. I was always amazed by how much he knew about what went on in this place. He knew about each one of us.

Over the past few months, Father Ron and I had become friends. I thought he might turn on me after I opened up to him, but he never did. It made me trust him.

As we walked, he told me he needed a special assistant and wondered if I was interested in the job. It would require me to greet visitors and run errands with him. He told me I had made an impression on him, especially in my willingness to help others. He said if I did a good job, I could eventually get my license and be his driver. The whole idea was so exciting I forgot all about Eva, the rehearsal and her trip.

Of course, I said yes. "I knew I'd chosen the right man for the job," he said as he patted me on the shoulder. And then, he did something that really affected me. He shook my hand and said, "Thank you Sammy. I'm looking forward to working with you when I return from the trip."

As he walked away, I felt something I hadn't felt in a long time, maybe not since I'd helped Jorge on the bread route, maybe never. I felt proud, and thanks to Father Ron, for the first time in my life, I felt like a man.

#

&

CHAPTER SEVEN

FATHER RON
TAKE OFF

I sat back, closed my eyes, took a deep breath and felt the pressure as it pushed my torso into the seat. For me, airplanes engage a sense of both excitement and fear. No matter how many times I fly, I'm always amazed at the sheer power of an airplane and the emotion it evokes. Maybe God is like that, a sense of power and peace at the same time; the confidence to let go combined with a fear of the unknown.

As we made our initial ascent, I peeked over at Juan, who was next to me, to see how he was holding up on his first flight. I couldn't remember how I felt my first time. When was it, anyway? Where did I go? Washington D.C. with a school group? A family trip to Florida?

Juan had his nose plastered to the window, and I was convinced if he could, he would hang his head out of the airplane. To say he was excited was an understatement. He was watching everything: the trucks, the baggage crew loading the suitcases, and now the ground disappearing as we took off. The plane banked right, and the ground filled the window. I looked away and grabbed the arm rest, as if holding on and leaning away would keep me safe.

Juan didn't flinch. He was taking it all in, happy as a clam. I guess after a life full of challenges and tragedies, one in which you are really never in control, the idea of flying seemed inconsequential.

I stayed silent and let him experience the moment on his own. Without legs, he was able to turn his entire body toward the window. The seat belt was draped across his stumps, and I wondered if it would do any good if we hit turbulence. His legs lay on the floor by my feet along with his polio-style crutches and pants. I was amazed and happy at how well he had adapted to the prosthetics we obtained for him after his arrival at NPH. For the trip, he wore comfortable shorts over his stumps. I was so happy about having him at NPH. I often thought of Maria and her words to me about Juan. I thought back to the day I first met him, with his shorts sweeping the dirt floor. It made me smile.

Dear God,
Sometimes I know I ask for too much.
Today, I say a prayer of thank you.
Thank you for delivering Juan to NPH.
And thank you for Maria, who pleaded for his future.
Thank you for the path that allowed us to accept him to the orphanage, and for the donors
making our trip to the U.S. possible.
And finally, Lord, thank you for Juan's music,
which has opened this door.
Thank you for bringing us so far.
Amen.

My mind went back to the day I was reunited with Juan on the streets. I was visiting a priest, Father Carlos, at his parish in San Salvador. Olegario had asked me to reach out to local parishes and establish a relationship because many of the *pequeños* who had left the home were in these parishes with the local priests. It was a way for us to keep in touch with these kids as they transitioned into their adult lives.

Luis was driving past a local market when I heard someone beating what sounded like drums. As it turned out, the drums were large buckets, and the drummer was Juan. He was older than when I had first met him, maybe 12, but it was him. There he sat, on the street playing for money, one step up from begging.

"Stop the car, Luis. I see someone," I said.

"No Padre. Not here. Too dangerous." Luis' tone was firm and direct.

"But I know that boy. Remember the one with no legs? We visited his mother many times, and then one day, the family had disappeared." I pleaded with Luis to stop, turn the car around and go back.

"No Padre. You are not safe here, and neither am I."

Luis didn't have to tell me as much. I knew it was a dangerous area. He drove on as I looked through the back window and watched Juan get smaller and smaller. I remembered the last time we stopped at Juan's house for a visit and found no one. The neighbors told me the mother had died. They didn't know where Juan had been taken, and the government had no record of him. There was no trail of admittance into the social services system or any orphanage. I had failed his mother, who had pleaded with me at every visit to take him to NPH. I accepted the fact that I would never see Juan again.

A short while later, Luis pulled the car through a gate. I had been replaying every discussion with Maria in my mind. It all seemed so vivid. I flexed my right hand, thinking about her grip, strong and convincing.

Father Carlos met us at the car. He ministered to a parish in San Salvador, and he and I met on a regular basis. Today, before our meeting, I pulled him aside to talk about Juan Manuel.

"Yes, I know the boy," he said. "His mother passed away about eight months ago, and he was placed with family members. They helped him for a while, but he couldn't work or contribute, so he has taken to the streets with the others." Father Carlos had many stories like Juan's. His parish worked to help the "street poor," but he was realistic about the limitations of what could be done.

"Can you bring him to me?" I asked.

"Can you take him at NPH?"

"I don't know. But I want to. And I want to talk with him."

In my heart, I knew I had to do something, but at that moment, I wasn't sure what "that" was. I had thought about Juan many times after the day we arrived at his home and found it empty. Sometimes, I'd wake up and feel his mother's hand holding mine, begging me to do something.

Even now, on the airplane, I found myself rubbing my hands together when I thought about it. It was as if Maria was right there with me, squeezing my hand, looking me in the eye, pleading with me to help her son.

That day, more than three years ago, when I returned to visit, Father Carlos had Luis drive us up and down the streets to find Juan. Locals knew Father Carlos when we stopped. On our third try, a man told us exactly where to go. As we turned the corner, there he was, banging away for anything people would drop in the small can that sat on the ground in front of him.

I stepped out of the car, and Juan recognized me. He was friendly, which surprised me.

"*Hola Juan.*"

"*Hola Padre.*"

"I heard about your mother. I am deeply sorry."

He looked down, "*Si.*"

I got down on one knee. "Where are you staying?" I asked.

Like most of the kids, Juan was full of pride. He explained his extended family had taken him in. He tried to convince me things were good, and that he was just out here playing for fun.

I knew better. He was dirty and thin. His t-shirt had holes in it. His hair was long and in need of a good wash.

"I come to Father Carlos' parish every other week, on Fridays," I explained. "Will you meet me there next time? I want to see you."

He nodded, thanked a local for putting a coin in his can, and returned to his buckets. I patted him on the shoulder and returned to the car.

A few weeks later, I was kneeling in prayer in Father Carlos' church. Suddenly, and quite unexpectedly, I saw a familiar face peaking from the floor around the end of the pew. It was Juan.

After that day, he met me at the church every two weeks. We talked, we prayed and most importantly, we stayed connected. In the meantime, I was working behind the scenes on his behalf. Father Carlos had reached out to social services. I had contacted Father Wasson in Mexico about this special case, asking him to talk to Olegario for me to see if something—anything—could be done to get Juan to NPH.

Olegario wasn't happy. I had circumvented the chain of command in my pursuit of Juan. I could feel his consternation the day we pulled into NPH. When Juan hopped down from the back seat, Olegario stood stone-faced, brows furrowed, arms crossed. The kids approached as they always do, but this time, they stopped and stared. No questions. No dancing. Nothing.

Juan stared right back. It was the first time I noticed his "edge" and his cynicism. He was unyielding and didn't greet them as he took in his new surroundings.

I remember my first of many conversations with Olegario and other staff in the months after Juan's arrival. It began with a discussion of "proper channels," and continued with, "he doesn't fit in" and "he is mean to the other children."

Juan was tough, and the time he'd spent on the streets made him even tougher. Since his arrival, he'd been caught stealing food from the kitchen. He refused to do his chores. The staff complained about how he treated other children. During discussions with the leadership, I could feel Olegario staring at me.

For weeks, I trailed Juan, and each time he got out of line, I would swoop in and calmly talk to him about his demeanor. He always promised to be better. But then, something else would happen, and we'd have the same discussion over and over. It was like banging your head against the wall. Finally, I came to grips with the fact that talking wasn't going to help. I needed to take action.

One evening, I found Juan sitting by himself, rhythmically tapping his fingers on a small table. "Come with me," I said and started to walk across the quad toward school.

"A donde vamos?" ("Where are we going?") Juan asked. I didn't answer, I just kept walking, and silently, I prayed.

Dear God,
Please let me deliver this message with meaning.
Give Juan the courage to change.
Amen.

I opened the door to the music room where Otoniel was waiting, sitting at a music stand in front of the room. Together, we had devised a plan, a last-ditch effort to reach Juan.

I stood next to Otoniel. "This is your final chance Juan," I told him. "You will join the band. You must fit in. You must practice and do whatever Otoniel asks." I had never spoken to Juan like this before. In fact, I had never spoke to any of the children like this.

After my performance, I stormed out the door into the hallway. I'm sure Juan thought I had left the building, but I waited outside the music room to listen to what would come next, hoping for a miracle.

"Welcome to the music room," Otoniel said. "Father Ron says you like to drum." Juan said nothing. After a long pause, Otoniel continued. "You are now a drummer and a member of the band. That means you must always respect this room and everything and everyone in it: the music, the instruments, your fellow musicians and me."

There was another long pause, and I quietly opened the door a crack to see what was going on. Otoniel was looking at Juan. Juan was looking at the floor. Finally, Juan looked up, and Otoniel continued. "You will come to music class with the others every day and return every evening to practice with me."

Juan didn't move as Otoniel disappeared into a back room adjacent to the music room. Moments later, he emerged with a set of drumsticks and gave them to Juan.

"These are yours," he said. "They have your name on them. Do not lose them." Hearing the gravity in Otoniel's voice, you would have thought he was handing Juan his firstborn child. Juan simply nodded.

I returned to my quarters that evening with no expectation this scheme would work or that Juan would change his ways. In fact, I was almost sure he wouldn't. Juan had thick skin from everything he had endured; not just the disfigurements he had since birth or the burn scars from the terrible fire, but the massive emotional walls he'd built around himself. His mother's death had been a great loss, but he had also endured the loss of his legs, the fire and the abandonment of this father. "What does that do to someone?" I thought. "Can we even reach him?" I fell asleep convinced that our efforts to get him involved in the music troupe was a fool's errand.

Luckily, I was wrong. In the coming weeks, I made a point to walk over to the school in the evenings and there would be Juan, banging on the drums. His strong hands moved quickly, his head bobbing in rhythm. He was sweating, evidence of the hard work he was putting in for Otoniel, the group, and hopefully, for himself. On a few occasions, I saw him strumming a guitar or playing the keyboard, but I made sure he never knew I was watching and listening.

Sometimes, as I leaned against the wall and listened, I would dream that he would use music to find a common ground, the "beat" that would propel him to another level in his life. Outside the music room, I never mentioned practice or talked to him about the role music played in his life. Occasionally, I'd ask him if he was enjoying his time with the group, and he always said yes.

The plane rocked again, and I opened my eyes. Juan was still staring out the window. Did the world seem big or small to him? Did he understand how small El Salvador is in relation to it? I always wondered how the children who were chosen for these trips interpreted the vast outside world compared to their life at NPH.

I looked down the aisle and saw the other children talking and laughing. The kids chosen for this troupe were some of the best we had at NPH. They were offered privileges for earning good grades, doing their chores, being well-behaved and working hard in music and dance classes. Juan was the wild card. His attitude didn't warrant a place in this group or on this trip, but his practice, love for music and natural ability helped convince Otoniel to give him a chance. He had made me promise to watch over Juan throughout our journey.

After a few minutes, I broke the silence. "What do you see, Juan?"

"I see heaven, *Padre*," he replied. "If I could reach out this window, I could touch it."

"You once told me you didn't believe in God or heaven," I replied. "Have your feelings changed?"

It took a moment for Juan to answer. I didn't know if what came next would be sarcastic or sincere.

"Maybe there is a God for some people, *Padre*, just not for me."

He turned back to the window. I desperately wanted to talk to him about what he had just said; to try and change his mind. I started to speak but stopped. I remembered his mother telling me the same thing, and I decided to give him more time. He looked back toward me. Maybe he was surprised when I didn't respond or take the bait he had thrown in the water.

"I believe God has a plan for you," was all I said.

A week later, I was walking down the tight aisle of a moving bus, holding on to each seat as I made my way to the front. It was a big, comfortable coach bus, and a relatively smooth ride when one is sitting, but when you're traveling with a load of excited pre-teens and teenagers, navigating the aisle can be quite an adventure. The space was filled with costume bags, drums and luggage. Otoniel was in the front seat, behind the driver, and I plopped down next to him.

"What did you think of today?" I asked.

"The kids are still making mistakes, ones I thought we corrected back home," he replied as he looked up from his clipboard. Otoniel took these shows seriously and expected perfection from his performers.

"I think the crowds loved it," I said, spinning the conversation toward the positive. "And, the group seems to get better with each performance. They'll continue to improve."

Otoniel looked down at his notes and nodded.

I found my briefcase and pulled out the paperwork. We had

one hour before we were to pull into the parking lot at St. Mary of the Woods parish. The NPH Chicago office had worked with the parish to assign host families for the kids during our stay.

For Juan's host families, I requested homes with minimal stairs. I also asked that the hosts in all three cities speak Spanish and were fully aware of his medical issues before they committed to hosting. Without his legs, he could startle someone who wasn't prepared. Juan had also resisted the requirement to learn English. In fact, he resisted almost everything, with the exception of playing music.

The kids began singing, and I turned to listen. I loved their collective energy. The excitement of the trip had not waned while we were in Minnesota and Wisconsin. In fact, it was contagious. I was tired from the performances and the long days in general, but their energy gave me strength. They started to sing the NPH song.

One family united,
Sharing our love,
Through the sorrow and the beauty,
NPH together,
Friendship forever.
Brothers and sisters for life.

The song was written years ago by four *pequeñas*, which is how we refer to our girls. It was such a beautiful tribute to the organization. Where would these kids be without NPH? On the streets? Begging? Prostituting? Dead?

I looked out the window. The houses along the freeway were huge by El Salvador standards; middle-class for Americans. The concept of abject poverty is so foreign to everyone I know in the States. I wondered if our visits helped people understand, bridging the gap between the haves, the have-nots and the extremely poor, like our kids. Before the bus stopped at the parish, I prayed.

Dear God,
Open the hearts of the people we meet in Chicago.
Help them see what I see in these children,
self-worth through love and family.
An education that brings about smart decisions.
And the chance to change a life forever.
Keep them safe, and guide them home to you.
Amen.

Much like in the other cities, the bus pulled up to the school and the host families were lined up on the sidewalk. Our schedule for the week was packed with daily performances at parishes throughout Chicago, but the kids would spend their evenings with these families. I wondered what impact the American hosts would have on the kids. Even more, I wondered how the kids would open the eyes of the families. Would it be a positive experience?

The children on the sidewalk looked excited; their parents nervous. I was sure they struggled with the thought of bringing these strange kids into their homes. I assumed each family had a desire to be open and give their children an experience with someone from a different culture. But I also assumed each family carried some doubt and fear as to whether the visiting children would be a good influence. I believe that every time two cultures touch, we lessen the mental divide between the "us and them," and the thought kept me positive about the experience.

Katherine was the first to greet us and give us instructions before we unloaded the kids. Once she was done, she turned to the sidewalk.

"Thank you all for this beautiful welcome. The NPH troupe has traveled from Minnesota after a week of performances, but the kids are ready to meet you and visit your homes. In a moment, I will ask them to come off the bus, but first I want to give you all a few tips and guidelines."

Katherine's tone was authoritative yet reassuring, "Just what these host families need," I thought.

Katherine continued, as though she'd done this thousands of times. "The kids have been assigned to your family in pairs. When they get to your home, spend some time introducing your family, show them their room, and explain how to use your bath and shower. They study English at school, but remember to talk slowly and don't be surprised if they don't understand every word. They may be hungry, so please offer them something to eat. I ask that you don't keep them up too late. They have had a big day and must be back here by 9:00 a.m. tomorrow, so they need to sleep. Also, please do not give them extravagant gifts. We do not have space to take large gifts home and only small things will fit in their suitcases. At NPH, the kids share everything. So, gifts of playing cards or games are great, but please don't give them electronics or other expensive items. And now, Father Ron will give us all a special blessing."

I stood on the bus steps and raised my arms, speaking loudly so everyone could hear: "Dear God, bless all the children here tonight; those visiting and those receiving. Bless the families who have so lovingly opened their homes and their hearts. Bless new friends and new experiences. Keep us all safe on our journey and be with us as we do our work in Chicago." I then repeated it all in Spanish.

Immediately following the blessing, Katherine began calling names, and the kids filed off the bus in pairs. Boris, the youngest dancer, came off carrying a large, stuffed wolf from his family in Minnesota. I just shook my head. We had already discussed the problem of taking it on the plane home, but he continued to carry it everywhere.

By my request, Katherine called Juan Manuel last. My first reason was logistical, without legs he was slow and could hold up the process. The second was emotional. I wanted to talk to his host family before he met them.

"Father Ron? I'm Mary Dobin." I recognized the name from the list. She was Juan's host mother. We shook hands before I introduced her to Juan.

"I believe someone talked with you about his medical issues, including his legs, correct?" I asked.

"Absolutely. No worries Father, I'm a nurse," she replied. After a bit more chit-chat, I excused myself to get Juan off the bus. Inside, he sat near the back, looking out the window, tapping his fingers on the seat in front of him. As I approached, he noticed me. "Let's go," I said, and he lifted himself off the seat and together, we made our way back to the parking lot where Mary and her husband were waiting.

"Mary, this is Juan Manuel." Before I could continue, Mary jumped in, speaking to Juan in Spanish. He held out his hand ever so slightly. It was the first time I'd seen him anything but confident, or more accurately, cocky. He was nervous.

The forearm brace from his polio crutch clung to his arm as Mary grabbed it with both hands. Her hands were so small and white compared to his. Mary smiled at him, and to my surprise, he smiled back. "Maybe this would work out better than it did with his host family in Minnesota," I thought.

Someone touched my shoulder, and I was reluctant to turn away. I wanted to make sure Juan's handoff went well. Then I realized it was Marlene Byrne, a host parent I had gotten to know during a planning event for the trip. She was in charge of host family coordination. Boris was standing next to her son, Matthew.

"Excuse me, Father Ron. I just wanted to say hello before we leave with the boys," she said as she motioned to the kids.

"So nice to see you again, Marlene," I replied. "I see Boris and Javier are staying with you. That's great."

"Yes. I think that wolf is bigger than he is," she said with a chuckle. I rolled my eyes, which made her laugh out loud.

"He's been told it will be an issue on the plane ride back. Apparently, our 'no large gifts' message wasn't too convincing in Minnesota," I replied with faux disgust.

After we finished talking, I turned to see how Juan Manuel had gotten on with his family, but they were already gone. In fact, all the cars had pulled away, and the parking lot was empty. I stood there quietly, exhausted, and excited for the kids but also nervous.

Moments later, I was back on the bus, waiting to be dropped off on the South Side to meet my own family. I should have been more excited to spend some time with the ones I loved in my childhood home but the thought of leaving NPH made me nostalgic. I looked back at the empty seats, that just an hour ago had been filled with so much life and joy.

I had an overwhelming feeling of sadness and began to reflect about my time at NPH. The children, the staff but even more, the mission had become part of my soul. After five years at NPH and away from the Chicago Diocese, the Cardinal had requested I return and take a new position with the church. He had called me home, but right now, it seemed more like I was being called away from my home. I couldn't decide.

I had not told anyone, not even my family, about my departure from El Salvador in 18 months. I couldn't imagine my life without the NPH kids and my work there.

#

♪

CHAPTER EIGHT

MARLENE
IT'S A TRAP

Boris and Javier were nearly the last names called. Boris jumped off the steps after peeking his smiling face out of the bus door. Javier followed close behind.

I got the opportunity to say hello to Father Ron before we gathered up the boys and my kids and headed for the car. On the short drive home, we realized Javier knew some English, and I decided to take full advantage.

"How was your trip?" I asked.

"Good, but big drive."

"It rained?" Brian chimed in to discuss the weather.

"*Sí*," Javier smiled.

Katherine had told all the families that the kids might not have great English skills, but she assured us we would find ways to communicate. Perhaps this would be easier than I thought.

I turned to the back seat again. "Boris, where did you get the Timberwolf?"

Javier answered. "It gift from family." He looked at Boris and spoke to him in Spanish. Boris shook his head and hugged the stuffed animal. As he turned back to me, Javier added, "But too big for plane."

At home, Matt jumped out of the van to carry Boris'

suitcase up the front stairs, talking a mile a minute. Boris was the youngest child in the music troupe, and I was happy to see the two of them bounding into the house together. Javier grabbed his own bag along with two garment bags. Clearly older than Boris, he was a handsome, courteous young man.

I turned to Javier. "Does Boris know any English?"

"Not too much, no."

As we entered the house, I noticed Boris was smiling at Matt. He hadn't spoken yet but seemed really happy to be here and with us. That was until he saw Murphy, our 95-pound Goldendoodle and turned to run out the door. Murphy took his duty as "guest greeter" seriously. From family and friends to complete strangers, he barked first and then turned to mush.

"He's fine, friendly," Matt said as he wrapped his arms around Murphy's neck and pushed him further into the house and away from our guests.

Boris was still standing out on the porch as Javier walked in, set down the cases and began to pet the dog. Brian nodded to Boris. "It's okay." Brian has an amazingly mild, comforting demeanor, and it was just what the doctor ordered amid the excitement and controlled chaos of the moment.

Brian took the boys upstairs to the guest room while I hung up their dance clothes in the front hall closet. Maggie was staying close to me. At five years old, this probably seemed very odd to her. She was curious but clearly not excited about having these strangers in her house.

"Let's get some snacks and sandwiches for the boys," I said as I grabbed her hand. The idea of snacks before bedtime was always good.

"Why can't Boris talk?" she asked as we prepared a tray of food.

"He can talk, honey. He just speaks a different language; Spanish. He doesn't understand English."

"How can he not understand when we talk? Even the dog understands," she replied.

I laughed at first, and then realized she could understand speaking another language but not the fact that someone could not comprehend her own. Maybe that's why adults tend to talk louder and slower when they first meet someone who speaks a different language.

I tried to explain it. "When I say words, they are in English. You understand those words because we talk and read in English. Boris only understands the words if you say them in Spanish."

Maggie looked at me, tilted her head and confidently replied, "Well he should watch *Dora the Explorer*. She could explain English and Spanish to him."

I was still laughing when Brian and the boys appeared in the kitchen.

"How are things upstairs?" I asked.

"I showed them everything. How to use the shower, where to find the towels and how to operate the lights," he replied. Katherine had asked the families to give the kids instructions about electricity, plumbing and the general layout of their homes because the kids don't have private showers and rooms at NPH.

"All good?" I asked Javier.

"Good, thank you," he replied with a big smile.

Matt and Boris bumped each other climbing onto the stools at our kitchen counter. They both laughed and dug into a big bowl of potato chips.

With his mouth full, Matt asked, "Can we go downstairs and play?"

"Yes, but only for a while. We all have to be up early."

Matt motioned to Boris and the two boys were off as quickly as they had arrived. Brian grabbed Maggie, who was unhappy she had to go to bed earlier than the boys. She never liked it when Matt was allowed special privileges because he was older.

That left Javier and me alone in the kitchen. As I began to clean up, he jumped up to help me. At first, I wanted to say he didn't have to, that he was our guest, but I decided to let him.

"Javier, do you like coffee?"

"Yes."

"Me too. Let's make some." I brought down two cups.

"Are you in high school?" I asked.

"Yes. I grade 10."

"How long have you lived at NPH?"

"Me and two sisters for eight years."

"How old are your sisters?"

"One 10. One 12."

"Are they in the troupe, too?"

Javier just stared at me, and I wasn't sure if he didn't understand, or if I had said something to upset him. I rephrased my question, "The music group?"

He started to nod, "No, just me. And I dancer." He sat up straighter.

"Really! That's awesome." In my head, I hadn't figured Javier for a dancer. Instead, I imagined him, like so many American teenage boys, being enamored with the guitar and rock music. I noticed his enthusiasm and pride for dancing.

"Your English is very good," I said.

"Not too good." He smiled. He seemed embarrassed.

"Where did you learn?" I asked.

"At NPH. We take class in school. Teacher make us talk."

We continued to talk until Javier finished his coffee. He jumped up to take the cup to the sink. I wanted to tell him to put it in the dishwasher, but I stopped. He immediately washed it with the hand soap on the counter, dried it and turned to put it back in the cabinet. I pointed to the cupboard door just right of the refrigerator. "Thank you," I said.

As I got up from my chair, I was afraid to put my dirty cup in the dishwasher, so I hand-washed mine as well and put it in the cupboard.

"Let's see what Boris and Matt are doing," I said.

I walked toward the basement door, and Javier followed me. I was about to yell down to the boys but heard them both talking at once. I looked back at Javier, putting my finger to my lips and motioning for him to follow me, and we descended the stairs in silence.

The two boys were struggling to put together the *Mouse Trap* game. Boris' large stuffed wolf was sitting on the floor next to them as if it were watching. The boys were jabbering back and forth at each other in English and Spanish. Neither seemed to notice the language barrier. Matt gestured what he wanted and Boris nodded and smiled a smile that made his entire face light up. Already, they had established a working relationship.

I looked back at Javier, laughing silently. I felt so happy. We both took another step and sat down on the stairs together to get a better look.

"The marble starts here. You put the chute on this stand then the marble will take off," Matt said.

Boris was talking in Spanish at the same time, *"Poner la chibola sobre la base que recorre la rampa hasta el final."*

"The angle gives it enough speed to roll through the chute and down the steps," said Matt, scooting on the floor to the other side of the structure.

Next, Boris chimed in: *"Debería ir lo suficientemente rápido para llegar a los pasos,"* (It should be going fast enough to reach the steps.)

"Javier, does Boris speak *any* English?" I whispered.

Javier shook his head. "He only know little words."

Together, the boys tipped the steel ball, and a chain reaction ensued. Within seconds, it was mission accomplished. The mousetrap fell. The boys cheered and high-fived.

Javier let out an appreciative laugh. *"Vamanos,* Boris."

Boris grabbed the stuffed wolf and shook Matt's hand before they both ran up the stairs past me. I just sat there, amazed.

As Brian came to bed that evening, I was lying still, smiling at the ceiling. "What are you thinking about?" he asked.

"Just how pure the boys were playing tonight. They can't talk to each other, but they can be friends. It's so weird, right?"

"Not really. Boris has a smile that would make anyone his

friend," Brian said from the bathroom. I thought the same about Javier. I feel like we really struck the jackpot with these two.

The next morning, the boys left early for a performance at another parish. As soon as I dropped them off, we resumed our regular school and work routine. The next two days were the same. Breakfast with the boys before we dropped them off at the NPH bus, then school for the kids. Then, we'd wait for the boys to return in the evening.

Finally, it was the night of the fiesta at our parish. Brian and I were in the kitchen. With no dinner to prepare (it was part of the fiesta), we were sitting at the counter, watching the clock. Javier was in the bedroom, and Matt and Boris were again playing in the basement.

Fascinated by their relationship, I silently crawled back down the basement stairs to watch. With pieces of blocks and trucks strewn all over the floor, they were building something, but I really couldn't tell what it was. Yet, they seemed fully content, both of them rambling on and on, as happy as could be.

I felt someone on the stairs and turned to see Javier behind me. I could sense he was nervous.

"Boris, *vamanos, ahorita mismo!*"

He looked at me, "We not be late."

Boris and Matt raced up the stairs. Matt looked at me, "Come on, Mom! The fiesta!" He said it as though he was the only one who knew what was happening.

I touched his arm. "Did you understand what he was saying?" I asked, referring to the pieces spread out across the floor.

"Not a word."

"But how did you...?"

"It's a game, Mom, you can't do it wrong. You just build it."

The school parking lot was full of minivans and SUVs, sitting in front of a large gymnasium attached to a school. Brian pulled up to the gym doors to let everyone out.

"Let's move boys, we don't want to be late!" he said.

The side van door slid open automatically, and before it opened all the way it stopped and reversed direction. Before it closed all the way it stopped again and went back to open. About halfway it stopped again. I realized it was not malfunctioning.

After a brief pause, the door continued to open. Boris peeked around the sliding door with a big smile on his face. Javier scooped him up from behind and jumped out of the minivan, carrying Boris under one arm and two garment bags under the other.

"Sorry Miss Marlene, he never see door like it before," he said as he headed for the gym.

"The wonders of modern technology," I said to Brian as the kids piled out. He shook his head, laughed and started to drive away.

Suddenly, Boris turned around and headed back toward the van. Matt cut him off and held out the large stuffed toy wolf he had left in the car. Boris smiled, took the wolf and shook Matt's hand.

Families milled about the gym, taking their seats at tables set up in front of a makeshift stage. Javier and Boris hurried through the front doors and hustled over to where some other children with garment bags had gathered. We headed in the opposite direction to find our assigned table.

As we were getting seated, you could hear the families comparing notes about their new guests. Father Don, an older priest in our parish, approached the microphone, tapped it to make sure it was "hot," and started to speak. "Thank you all for coming this evening. My dear friend, Father Ron Hicks, has brought a group of talented children from Nuestros Pequeños Hermanos orphanage in El Salvador to perform for you this evening. Father Ron is the director of the home and three others across Central America. His work allows the children to live as a family, go to school and work toward a better future. Please join me in welcoming Father Ron."

The room filled with applause as Father Ron walked from the back of the room and took the stage. I noticed the NPH kids clapping louder than all of us. They loved him so much, and it showed.

"We are very excited to perform for you this evening with a special presentation of El Salvadoran music and dance," he said.

As Father Ron continued, a boy with two polio-style crutches made his way to the stage and sat behind the drum set.

"The musicians and dancers you will see tonight are all part of the school music program at Nuestros Pequeños Hermanos, or NPH, as we affectionately call it. Led by our music director, Otoniel, these students were selected to train for our travel troupe and given this special privilege to perform in the United States."

There was polite applause from the crowd. The boy with the crutches had taken his position on a stool behind the drum kit. I noticed he was tapping his lap with his hands, as though he was practicing one of the numbers in his head.

Father Ron concluded his brief introduction. "I'm so happy to introduce to you our Nuestros Pequeños Hermanos music and dance troupe!" Everyone clapped as the other musicians joined him on stage.

The drummer lifted his sticks. *"Uno, dos, tres…"*

At the other end of the gymnasium, dancers appeared in colorful costumes and waded into the audience, making their way toward the center of the floor. When the music started, so too did the dancers, clapping with the beat and encouraging the audience to join in.

It didn't take much. Children and adults alike were amazed. Everyone rose to their feet cheering, eager to join in. The young children were sitting on the ground circling the dance floor, trying to get close to the action. When Boris danced past our table, he leaned down and gave Matt a high-five.

For more than an hour, the troupe danced and played before the dancers left the floor briefly, only to emerge in colorful, new costumes.

The grand finale.

The girls twirled in long, brightly-colored skirts, theatrically raising one side up high as they danced. The entire room could feel the happiness of the musicians and dancers. Toward the end of the final song, the dancers grabbed guests to participate. Javier grabbed me to dance and I did my best to follow his lead and mimic his movements.

When the concert was over, the troupe members left to change, returning to the gym to mingle with the crowd. Katherine walked over to our table.

"Marlene, thank you for your work coordinating the host families," she said. "I think everyone is doing really well here."

"I know," I said. "The kids don't seem to have any language barrier. Boris and Matt are having a great time playing."

"And what about you? Are you feeling the kids' presence?" she asked.

"Yes. It's incredible to hear their stories. You all do such fantastic work," I replied.

"I'm so glad you think so because I want to talk with you about being on our Board here in Chicago."

"Me?"

"Don't answer tonight. I'll reach out and give you more information about what it entails. But I think you would be a great addition to our fundraising efforts."

I was still thinking about the conversation as we headed to the car.

"That performance deserves ice cream," Brian said. Our kids yelled back in agreement, and I could see Javier smile. He leaned over and whispered to Boris, "*Sorbete.*"

As we circled the drive-thru, Boris climbed up near Brian's ear, poking his head through to watch him order. At first, I thought he wanted something, but soon I realized that he had never seen a drive-thru window. He stayed there, mesmerized as they handed ice cream out the restaurant window, then leaned out even further to see what was inside. What did he think about someone handing food through the window of a building into a car?

On the ride home, I felt a deep sense of happiness. "This has been fantastic," I said, half to myself and half to anyone who could hear.

"Yes, fantastic," Brian replied. I could tell he was only half listening.

I continued. "The kids really enjoyed it."

"Really enjoyed it."

"Maybe we can do it again sometime."

"Yes, let's do it again." Brian has a knack for being part of the conversation without fully concentrating on it.

"Boris and Javier are having such a great time staying with us, so…" I whispered. "What if we could extend it? What if we could adopt?"

This got his complete attention, and his head swiveled with a wide-eyed look. "What?"

I knew my emotions had gotten the best of me. I also knew NPH did not allow adoption but my emotions were palpable.

"Let's talk later," Brian said. I continued to lick my ice cream cone. On the inside, I realized I liked the idea of being in these kids' lives. This was their final night with us, and it made me sad. I had a deep pull to stay connected.

The next morning, we lined up on the curb, Matt, Boris, Maggie, me, Brian and Javier, with suitcases, two garment bags and a stuffed wolf. For once, I hated the fact that I was always early for things. The bus was waiting, but we were one of the first families to arrive, and it was awkward. We didn't want to see Boris and Javier get on the bus, and we certainly didn't want to say goodbye. I didn't want to cry, and I kept telling myself to keep my emotions in check.

Within 15 minutes—which seemed like an eternity—cars began pulling into the lot. Everyone was moving slowly. Finally, Otoniel broke the silence, "Let's start loading the luggage."

Matt pulled Boris' luggage, as Boris struggled to hold up the garment bag while carrying his stuffed wolf.

"You want me to put this in the luggage bin under the bus?" Matt asked.

"*Solo pongo mi valija en el autobus,*" (Just put my luggage in the bin under the bus.) Boris replied. I smiled, realizing the boys were parroting one another in English and Spanish.

Matt loaded the luggage, then put out a hand for Boris. Boris started to shake Matt's hand but couldn't help himself. He pulled Matt close for a big hug.

"*Fue un placer conocerte Matt. Gracias por hacerme sentir como en casa*" (It was nice to meet you, Matt. Thank you for making me feel so happy.) Boris stepped back, and both boys tried to put on a brave face.

Boris smiled wide, and said a single word in English, "Mousetrap."

Matt laughed. It eased the tension.

Boris walked over to Maggie and me, giving us "fly-by" hugs as he dashed off to the bus, hiding his tears. Javier started to hug me when he noticed Boris still had the stuffed wolf.

"That dog!" he said as he followed Boris.

Boris ducked past Father Ron, who was standing near the bus door. Javier bounded onto the bus after him.

Father Ron stepped up to see what was going on. We could hear Javier and Boris scuffling and arguing on the bus. Several troupe members, still outside the bus, craned their necks to get a look at what was going on. Soon, Javier and Boris calmly walked off the bus. Boris still had his stuffed wolf. They walked over to us.

"He gives it to you, Matt. He can no take on plane," Javier said.

Boris held it out to Matt, looking down at the ground.

"But you got that in Minnesota. It's the Timberwolf. I can't." Matt looked to Brian and me.

Boris looked Matt in the eye. *"Me lo dieron esto en Minnesota. Es el Timberwolf. Quiero que lo tengas,"* (I got this in Minnesota. It's the Timber Wolf. I want you to have it.).

"If it's too big for the plane, could I mail it to him?" Matt asked Brian.

"I don't think so," Brian answered.

"Too big." Boris continued, and pushed the animal toward Matt. Brian simply put a hand on Matt's shoulder and nodded. Finally, Matt reached out and took it. Boris hugged him tightly, then bowed his head and ran toward the bus. At the bus door, Boris looked back to Matt and the stuffed wolf one more time, tears welling up in his eyes.

I didn't know what to do. I looked down as Matt held the animal. I could see tears rolling down his cheeks, and it set off my emotions. Brian put his arm around me as I leaned into his shoulder, crying as hard as anyone in the parking lot that morning; and there were a lot of us.

My next comment came out of nowhere. "I think we should take the kids to El Salvador."

Brian looked at me like I had gone crazy. Thankfully, he said nothing. He just packed it away in that part of his brain reserved for "conversations best had at a later date."

As the bus pulled away, I noticed Maggie. She was waving, unaffected. When the bus turned the corner, she looked up at me and then to Matt. "Why are you crying?" She shrugged and headed toward the car.

#

CHAPTER NINE

FATHER RON
IN YOUR FACE

I should be exhausted after two weeks of traveling, but watching the show finale for the last time renewed my energy. All the audiences loved the performances, excitedly clapping and swaying to the music, at times even dancing, and tonight was no different. I watched the kids grab audience members, pulling them to the center of the floor to participate.

I was relaxed and leaning against the gymnasium wall as Father Don Headley approached. He's an elderly priest who shuffles with purpose. I knew Father Don from his work in Panama. He had lived there for many years before returning to Chicago to retire.

"Father Ron, meet Doctor Patel," he said abruptly. I reached out to shake his hand. "Doctor Patel is a surgeon at Shriners Hospital here in Chicago. I've invited him and his wife to be our guests tonight. I told him he needed to meet you and see these kids, especially Juan Manuel."

"It's a pleasure to meet you, doctor. How long have you worked with Shriners?"

"Let's see," he thought for a moment, then smiled. "I guess it's been almost 10 years. I volunteer, performing surgery one day a week." It was obvious he had a deep commitment to his work with Shriners.

"Not only is he a surgeon there, he's on the Board of Directors," Father Don added.

"How many children do you serve?" I asked.

"Nationally, we treat thousands of children each year. Here in Chicago, I specialize in craniofacial and plastic surgery. Don has told me about the fantastic work you do with these kids." We glanced over at the dancers.

"Thank you. Sometimes I think they do more for me than I do for them," I replied.

Never taking his eyes off the troupe, Doctor Patel continued, changing the subject. "Father Ron, I was wondering why the drummer has not had his cleft palate repaired."

I nodded. "Juan Manuel. His cleft is severe, and he came to us at an older age, about 12. The doctors in El Salvador don't have the capacity to repair it. Also, we don't have the funds. Even *Doctors Without Borders* declined him."

"I see. Does he show complications from his cleft?" he asked.

"Do you mean health issues?"

"Yes. Some patients have health problems related to the condition."

"Juan has had some nasal infections, but amazingly, very few problems and no voice issues. He speaks well and sings clearly," As I spoke, Juan was beating the drums like he'd been born with sticks in his hands.

Doctor Patel continued. "Really? And his legs?"

"He was burned as a young child, and they had to amputate to save him."

Doctor Patel shook his head, I'm sure thinking what everyone who had heard even a small part of Juan's story thought. "Amazing." Doctor Patel gave Father Don a look. I wasn't sure what it meant, but it felt like they were up to something. Before I could find out, the music stopped and the loudspeaker kicked in.

"And now, Father Ron Hicks will close the night's festivities." With that, I shook both men's hands and made my way to the stage.

The next morning, I was feeling somber as Otoniel and I

stood next to the bus watching the cars arrive to drop off the kids for the trip home. He seemed relieved and ready to conclude what had been a successful—albeit exhausting and sometimes tense—trip. But today, there was a slower pace. The fiestas were over and, as with all vacations, the trek home was never as exciting as the journey here. For the families that hosted children, there were so many new emotions. It never failed to amaze me how people fell in love with our children in the short time they were together, making goodbyes difficult. From my observations, most times it was harder for the families than the children, who were accustomed to leaving or being left behind.

The kids loaded their bags under the bus, but today, there was no hurry to board. Feeling the weight of leaving, after stowing their luggage, they returned to their host families. No one really knew what to do next. There is no script for how to leave someone, especially when, in all likelihood, you'll never see them again. The girls—always open to showing their feelings—hugged their host families. I saw Boris holding his big stuffed wolf. I knew I'd have to be the one to tell him he couldn't take it on the plane (a small cross to bear under the circumstances).

Over my shoulder, I saw Juan with his host family. He was standing next to them, but they were not talking. I could feel the tension as I approached.

"Mary. Jesse. How are you?" I asked.

"Good Father," Jesse replied.

I turned to Juan, "Did you enjoy Chicago?"

"Sí Padre," he replied.

Juan saw the others heading to the bus. He turned to Mary and Jesse, "Adios." He walked to the bus. I looked down, his suitcase still sitting at our feet. Juan's disability meant he needed help, but sometimes he used it as an opportunity to coerce others to do things for him. I couldn't decide if his attitude came from arrogance or if he liked the power of it all. But I did know there was a lack of appreciation, and that was unacceptable. I apologized to Mary and Jesse. Jesse picked up the bag and walked to the bus.

As I approached Marlene and her family to say thank you and

goodbye, I could see she was crying, and I smiled at the effect these days and events had on people. The realization for the host parents was that these children had none of the things their own children took for granted, and it overwhelmed them. That, coupled with the goodbyes, made emotions run deep.

I rubbed Marlene's arm as I walked past but said nothing. I turned my attention to the ruckus on the bus but before I could board, Boris climbed down the steps. I watched him walk over to Marlene's son, Matthew. Though Boris was two years older than Matthew, they were the same height. Our kids were always small for their ages due to a combination of genetics and the lack of early nutrition. Boris handed the big wolf to Matthew and then hugged him, sandwiching the stuffed animal between their bodies. Tears ran down Matthew's cheeks as Boris hugged Marlene again before returning to the bus.

It was time.

An hour later—and after what seemed like a full day's work—I was walking to the taxi stand at O'Hare. I had helped the team get the kids from the bus through security. Now, I was headed back to my parent's home. As I waited in line, I found myself thinking about the bus ride here. I had made my way to the back of the bus, where I found Juan sitting alone. I silently sat down next to him. His head was turned away from me as he watched the traffic. After a few moments, I broke the silence.

"Juan." He turned his head quickly as I spoke to him in Spanish. "I have a new word for you. I'm not sure if you know it, but I want you to take it home and practice."

He looked puzzled.

"The word is 'gratitude'."

I could see this word made him uncomfortable. He whispered, "I know that word."

"Then I want you to start to think about it when you're around others."

He adjusted in his seat and looked down. For a few moments, we sat in silence.

"I didn't ask for this," he said quietly, looking down.

His words upset me, and I struggled to keep my voice down and our conversation private. "No, but your mother did, so be grateful to her and for her, even if you're not grateful for every opportunity you've been given." He was shocked by my anger.

I don't like the discipline side of this job. Most of the time, I leave it to someone else. I always question whether I am saying the right thing to make an impact on the kids, or if they take me seriously when I scold or reprimand them.

With nothing else to say to Juan, I got up quickly and headed to the front of the bus.

Today, I was glad I didn't have to fly all the way to El Salvador sitting next to him. I hoped I'd given him something to think about.

I spent the evening with my family. It always feels comforting to be home, regardless of how old you are or how long you've been away. Family photos on the shelves. Eating off the dishes you used as a child. Simply being around those people who know you best. It was just what I needed at that moment.

I didn't think about Juan again until later that evening, when I looked at my watch and realized the troupe had landed in El Salvador. I thought about the chaos at the airport, loading them onto buses with all their luggage and the long ride back to the NPH home.

Dear God,
Open his heart.
Give me the right words and actions to reach him before it's too late.
If not me, then deliver someone else who can.
Amen.

#

♪

CHAPTER TEN

SAMUEL GREEN

The weeks were hard while Eva was gone. But I kept thinking about our last few minutes together the night before she left, and that made it easier. I thought about her all the time. One day, some of the kids caught me daydreaming and laughed at me. I was thinking about what things would be like when the bus came through that gate and we were together again.

I couldn't wait to tell her my good news. I had registered for driver's education and was reading about how to drive a car. Father Ron said I might be able to get behind the wheel for the first time in a few months.

But what I expected and what I saw when the group returned were two different things. The bus arrived around 2:00 p.m. Everyone was expecting them, and as soon as we heard the gate, we all ran out to meet them. The singers and dancers got off two buses, smiling and laughing, everyone hugging. One by one, I watched them and waited. I didn't see Eva. Then, after the others had gotten off, I saw her. I saw *them.*

She was with Juan. They were smiling and laughing as they got off the bus together. She was helping him with his bag. He was loving the attention.

Even from this far away, I noticed it. Her wrist was empty. The bracelet was gone. She had promised to wear it. Immediately I was bitter, thinking about Juan spending all those days with her, once again getting his way because of his physical conditions, using his power to manipulate. I knew it was wrong to have those thoughts about someone who'd had the struggles he had. But I also knew how he played people, and now he had played Eva. I turned and went back to my dorm.

At dinner, Otoniel got up to report on the trip. The entire troupe stood at the front of the room as he talked about their wonderful performances, and how well everyone had gotten along with their host families. I knew it was an important opportunity for sponsors to help our home. Everyone knew it. And the kids who had traveled were proud of their work.

As Otoniel spoke, I couldn't take my eyes off Eva. "I couldn't be prouder of all of you for the way you represented NPH," he said, but I barely heard his words. I was too caught up in my own anger and jealousy.

Juan was up front too, twirling his drumsticks. "Show off," I thought. He was perched on a stool, and as Otoniel talked he took fake bows, out of Otoniel's sight. All eyes were on Juan, including Eva's.

After dinner, I went to the dishwashing station to do my chores. Eva was in the kitchen too, but I didn't look at her. I avoided her by volunteering to wipe down tables in the cafeteria.

In the far corner, I saw Otoniel and Juan sitting together. Otoniel was holding Juan's drumsticks in one hand, a green notebook in the other. It looked serious.

I kept my head down but got closer, wiping a nearby table. "The music would be nothing without me. You need my talents." Juan's words matched his attitude: cocky. Otoniel seemed stunned.

Even I was surprised by Juan's words, and for a moment, I stopped working to listen closer. Juan saw me. "What are you looking at?" I hadn't realized I was so close to them.

I immediately hurried off, and as I came through the door to the kitchen, I ran right into Eva.

"Why are you ignoring me?" she said, and I could tell she was upset.

"Why do you like Juan?" I shot back. "He's not what you think."

"Me like Juan? What do you mean?" She started laughing.

"You're not wearing my bracelet."

"You mean *my* bracelet?" she said as she pulled it from her pocket. Then, she turned and stormed away. I realized I had been wrong and chased her out the door, yelling her name. Finally, she stopped, and I caught up to her, apologizing like I had never apologized to anyone before. After a moment, she smiled and gave me a playful push on my chest.

"Tell me about the trip," I said, and for the next hour, we sat on the grass outside the mess hall and talked about her trip, my new job and before I knew it, we were friends again.

As it turned out, I was wrong about Eva. She never liked Juan. She didn't dislike him either. Just like the others, she felt sorry for him. I wasn't sure that was how he saw their relationship, but I didn't care. She liked me, and that was all that mattered.

I was so happy walking back to my dorm later that evening, I almost didn't see him. Juan was sitting outside, under a tree without his legs. He was alone, writing in the green notebook Otoniel had handed him in the mess hall. He never looked up at me, just kept scribbling. I wondered what he was doing, and if this was some sort of punishment. But I wasn't going to waste my time asking.

#

CHAPTER ELEVEN

FATHER RON
WHAT IF HE DOESN'T

I rarely used the desk in my office. Like most things at NPH, it was old and secondhand. Little more than a metal box, it had a second drawer that didn't close flush with the other two. It took me months to train myself not to hit my shin every time I went to sit down. Instead of sitting behind it when people visited, I typically formed a circle of chairs, and I'd sit beside the desk, using it as an elbow rest or a place to set my coffee.

For today's meeting, I arranged things differently. I decided to put myself behind the desk, in a power position. Olegario wasn't happy about my plan to take Juan to the United States for surgery, but he agreed that if I could convince the staff—our doctor, the social worker and the school principal—he would give me his support.

I knew there would be resistance. I knew it the moment Father Don spoke to me about the opportunity a month ago. He had called me at my parent's house prior to my return to inform me about the "plan" for Juan. How Dr. Patel had engaged Shriners in his case. It was a stretch and gave me a sinking feeling the entire flight back to El Salvador.

I felt my face turning red when I presented it to Olegario after my return to NPH. And I felt a deep sense of fear about discussing it in this office. I needed to be prepared, confident and authoritative.

In the States, I had tried to explain to Father Don why we might not be able to get the staff to agree to the idea, but my words fell on deaf ears. Father Don was steadfast, making a solid case for why it not only should happen, but why it *must* happen. I wished I could command a room like he did. More than that, I wished he could be here for this meeting. I felt the pressure of being the monkey in the middle of this message, trying to communicate and balance the fierce convictions of Father Don and the doctors in the U.S. against those of the NPH staff here in El Salvador.

I looked at the clock. I had 10 minutes. I rearranged the chairs again.

Liliana, the principal of our grammar school, entered the office first, which was a relief. She respected what I did in the school and was my strongest advocate in this group. We sat down in front of my desk and talked about the U.S. trip and some of the new students at the school.

It was my practice to search out new *pequeños* in the first few weeks after their arrival and connect with them through "random" meetups on campus. But it was never really random; I always had a strategy. I would find kids when they were in transition from one activity to another and "coincidentally" bump into them after a soccer match or in the cafeteria line where they couldn't scurry away. Through these encounters, I could get a feel for their transition and disposition without making it feel like a formal interrogation.

The kids with open demeanors were easy to spot. They looked at me and engaged when I asked them questions. It was the shy, angry or fearful kids that posed the greatest risk for not assimilating into school or life in the home. These kids were a puzzle and desperately needed our attention. Sometimes, their personalities would be the underlying cause of their ambivalence, but most often, it was a history of abuse, poverty, neglect or even malnutrition that affected them. Building trust—enough for them to understand they were safe—could be difficult, and it took time and attention. But without trust, we couldn't help these kids.

You'd think being a priest would be enough to foster some level of trust for these kids, but that wasn't always the case. The "collar" could make the relationship could go either way. Some were more respectful because of my status; others grew more distant. I had always struggled deciding how to dress. Do I wear the collar or dress more like the teachers and staff?

For the most part, I didn't wear it except at Mass. Sometimes, I wore it for one-on-one meetings with *pequeños* who were in real trouble. The respect for church and God ran deep in this country, even with the impoverished families. The most difficult children seemed to sit a bit taller and more attentive when I reminded them I was a man of God.

After changing my mind a few times, I had chosen to wear my collar for this meeting. I noticed Brenda, the administrator, was surprised and gave me a second look when she entered my office. She was too polite to say anything and was just there to listen and report back to Olegario and was quietly sitting in one of the chairs when Doctor Max entered.

He looked tired, but that wasn't unusual. Besides managing the health of all 476 children at NPH, his team had been caring for Christian, a chronically-ill, 12-year-old boy, whose body was ravaged by an aggressive virus. He was bed-ridden without much chance for a cure. Doctor Max had taken him to the hospital and confirmed a diagnosis of Chikungunya, which is transmitted to humans by mosquitoes. Symptoms include fever and severe joint pain, among a host of others.

Christian and his constant need for medical attention had taken a toll on the entire medical team.

"Why all the mystery, Father Ron?" Doctor Max asked as he sat down. His eyes told me he didn't want to be at this meeting, whatever the topic.

Before I answered, and just as Anita—our lead social worker—entered, I moved behind the desk. Anita was noisy and disheveled, carrying a pile of file folders; another staff member who had too many irons in the fire but no earthly way to catch up without more hands, brains or bodies to help her. I knew she would be my most important vote, so I let her get settled before I began.

I talked slowly (more for my sake, so I could stay calm and on task), giving them the whole story. I told them about Father Don and how he had introduced me to Doctor Patel at the Chicago fiesta and presented Juan's situation. I told them that doctors had discussed Juan, and felt they could fix his cleft palate. That Shriners Hospital had agreed to take him as a patient free of charge.

I paused and took the temperature of the group. "At least they seem engaged in the story," I thought to myself.

Next, I explained how I'd forwarded Juan's medical records to the U.S. I knew that would get a look from Doctor Max so I kept talking, picking up speed before he could interrupt. Also, I was afraid to stop for fear of losing my momentum and my confidence. I could see them all adjusting in their chairs and glancing at each other.

After sharing a few more details to bolster my case, I concluded my presentation. "This is an opportunity we cannot say no to," I said with as much authority and conviction as I could muster. "I'm asking for your support in offering this incredible gift to Juan Manuel." No one spoke, and I was tempted to continue talking, but I didn't. I simply waited. "Now, it's their turn," I thought as I sat quietly, breathing deeply to remain calm. I felt my collar digging into my neck. Looking down, I noticed my foot tapping quickly. Although they couldn't see it, I made a conscious effort to stop tapping, but it was difficult.

Doctor Max looked side to side, trying to get a feel from the others. After what seemed like an eternity, he spoke. "Father, this is a very nice gesture on their part, but we have to consider Juan's issues. His disability alone prevents us from sending him to the U.S.—through airports unaccompanied—for multiple surgeries. How would he navigate with prosthetic legs? What if he gets lost? Or worse yet, what if a bad guy preys on him? He has no way to protect himself."

Lilliana was next to chime in. "Let's add to that the fact he has resisted learning English in school. How would he communicate?"

Again, Doctor Max. "Juan's cleft palate is complicated. We've had *Doctors Without Borders* and top surgeons here in El Salvador refuse to treat him because of the number and sophistication of operations necessary to rebuild his face."

"Are you suggesting he move to the United States?" Anita asked. Technically, it was a question, but I heard it as, "He can't move to the United States."

The questions were coming all at once. I had completely lost control of the room. It seemed each of them had their own agenda and their own independent argument with me. The body language in the room, combined with the tone of their voices, made me realize I was losing the fight.

Finally, I held up my hand, breaking into Anita mid-comment. "Let's take one issue at a time," I said.

Anita sat back in her chair and crossed her arms. "First," I began, "he would not live in the U.S. They have secured a sponsor to pay for his flights back and forth from NPH for surgery and recovery at each phase." Silence from the crowd. I was regaining control.

"Second, Shriners has a craniofacial specialty team that takes on difficult cases like Juan."

"But what if there are complications?" asked Doctor Max.

"Max, you will have regular communication with the doctors at Shriners. They have assured me you would be part of the care team," I replied. "And Juan would recuperate at a host home before they release him to fly home to us."

Anita sat up and moved forward in her chair. "Father, with all due respect, you know Juan. What host family will be able to handle him? It's one thing treating a boy after surgery, but Juan has no legs, no English skills and a huge attitude." Anita was making good points, but I didn't concede anything. I just listened. She continued. "You have not even had success with him connecting to the families housing him for a few days during the fiestas. What makes you think this will be different, and over a longer period of time?"

"When we select families, I will personally make them aware of his challenges," I said. "I will also be making regular trips to Chicago to monitor the situation." Until that moment, I didn't realize the advantage this would give me in keeping my transfer back to the Chicago Archdiocese confidential.

For the first time in the meeting, Brenda spoke. "Do you have commitments from any families yet?" She was challenging me, thinking that fact alone could close this case. I simply shook my head, and as I was about to speak, Anita broke in.

"Families? Plural?" Anita asked. "Are you actually considering moving him around, living house-to-house during these recovery times?"

I took another deep breath, trying to find some inner strength. "Father Don has assured me he will find a host family that can do the lion's share of the work. Other families will be asked to help," I replied, feeling my confidence returning. I continued. "Father Don is realistic about Juan's challenges and personality. He will find the right family to take care of him. And he will be there to support them."

I pulled on my collar, wishing again that I had dressed more casually for the meeting. I might be losing the argument, but I was nowhere near giving up. Sitting back in my chair, I decided to tell a story.

"Doctor David Reisberg, a Chicago prosthodontist who is on the Shriner's team, heard about Juan, and he also saw obstacles as he considered the case. But on the very day he was looking through Juan's file and information, he noticed a business card he'd been given more than a year prior at a charity golf outing. 'This guy was in my foursome that day,' the doctor told me 'and I told him about my work at Shriners. After the round, the guy gave me his business card and told me to call him if I ever had a tough case that needed more help than Shriners could provide.' The doctor told me the man was from the Mulliganeers, a group of Chicago-area business people who wanted to pool their philanthropic dollars for charities geared toward children."

Finally stopping to take a breath, I noticed I had not only captured the group's attention but also regained control of the meeting.

"Anyway, I think it's interesting that Doctor Reisberg had

tossed that card on his desk where it floated around for more than a year. Then, on the very day he heard about Juan, the card resurfaced right there in front of him. I have to believe that's more than just a coincidence. The next morning, he called the man, telling him about Juan and asking if they might consider supporting the travel necessary for him to fly back and forth for a series of treatments."

I stopped, creating a dramatic pause before concluding the story. "And the Mulliganeers said yes."

Sensing a swing to my side, I was on a roll and kept rambling. "Is it God's plan? Is it something else? I don't know," I said. "But it's one more piece of the puzzle. From Juan's arrival, to his ability to play the drums to the connection at the fiesta, things just seem to be falling into place."

Everyone sat quietly. It was finally their turn to talk.

Brenda was the first to chime in. "What does Juan think about all this? Does he even want to do it?"

I had to admit I hadn't talked with Juan. They looked at each other and seemed to relax, figuring Juan wouldn't go for it and the issue might just fizzle out on its own. So, they gave me the green light to talk with him but not to promise anything. I took it as a good sign the team was open to the opportunity but knew I had to have a real heart-to-heart with Juan. And that wouldn't be easy.

We decided to reconvene after I had spoken to Juan. I was sure they were all hoping he would be against the whole thing. He was frequently against new ideas, and this one involved a significant commitment, and likely, a good amount of pain and rehabilitation.

After a day or two, I regained my nerve and called Juan to my office. I was again behind the desk with my collar on. This had to be a serious conversation. I worried he wouldn't comprehend the opportunity or its impact on his life. I needed to stress how important it was to have his full buy-in.

Juan scooted into my office and lifted his torso onto the chair in front of my desk. Although he had prosthetic legs, most days he chose not to wear them and would scoot on his stumps, using his hands to propel himself forward. I was always amazed to see him playing soccer with the other kids, using the backs of his hands to "kick" the ball. He was surprisingly quick and actually very competitive.

As Juan sat in front of me, I realized that I hardly noticed his facial deformities anymore. But now, as I focused on his open lip, mangled teeth and flat nose, I questioned the feasibility of all the procedures he'd need. Both Doctor Patel and Doctor Max had confirmed the severity of Juan's cleft palate. As I looked at him, I recognized the daunting task of reconstructing his face. It put a pit in my stomach.

"Will I look normal?" was Juan's first question after I explained the surgeries to him. He was touching his face as he asked.

"Yes Juan. They will fix your lip, nose and teeth," I confirmed. "But it's not only the look of your face, it will stop all the ear infections and congestion, making it easier to breathe, talk and eat."

"My teeth? How?" he asked.

"They will build a roof to your mouth much like mine." I showed him the top of my mouth. "Then, they will put in new teeth, called implants."

"What do they do with my old teeth?" His questions gave me confidence that we were making progress.

"They will be removed," I answered.

"But what do they do with them?"

I had no idea. "I guess they just throw them out," I replied.

Juan kept touching his lip and nose. I wondered if he was excited about the opportunity or worried about these major changes.

"Most important, Juan, is that you have to commit to this medical program. I'm not going to lie to you, there will be pain. And, it will mean traveling back and forth to the U.S. multiple times. It will mean listening to a team of doctors there—and Doctor Max here— and doing exactly what they ask. It will mean you have to be kind to your host family when you're in the U.S., no matter how long you're there or how difficult this gets. That gratitude I spoke to you about on the bus in Chicago? Now is the time to show it." I stopped for effect, the only sound in the room the ticking of the second hand on the big wall clock. "And, you must commit to all this. It could take up to two years, and there will be no turning back."

Juan sat silent. For once, he didn't have a smirk on his face or a flippant comeback. I hoped he was taking it all in. He started to speak, but I held up my hand to stop him.

"Juan, I don't want an answer today," I said. "I want you to pray on it and think about the opportunity you have before you. It's your decision, but if you agree, you must agree to it all."

After a moment, I told him he could go, and he should come back to me with his answer or any questions he had. As he scooted across the floor, I walked him out and watched him hurry across the grass to his dorm. Over the past 30 minutes, my emotions had been a rollercoaster, and now, I was less confident than ever. Was I doing the right thing? Could the surgeries really fix his face? Would he really be able to handle all this?

Part of me wished Father Don had never proposed the idea. So much was out of my control, yet I felt responsible for Juan and accountable to the team at NPH. My hand felt tight, like someone was squeezing it. I looked down at my palm, saw nothing and shook it out. I immediately remembered my time with Juan's mother, Maria.

Sometimes, when I would pray, I'd picture that green plaster ceiling in my first room at NPH. I seemed to always be praying to it when I first arrived. Olegario had given me new housing, but that night, I walked back into that room and looked up.

Dear God,

Find the center of Juan's heart,

And give him the strength to reach for this gift.

Help him learn to open up and trust,

So this opportunity gives him more than just a new face,

But also a deeper understanding of thankfulness and care for others.

And if this gift is not meant to be,

Give me the strength to accept it.

Bring your gentle touch to those I serve.

Amen.

The next week, I was back for another round with the staff. We all took our places at the chairs I had again arranged in a semi-circle around my desk. I felt more prepared this time, but before I could even thank them for taking time to reconvene, Anita launched right in.

"We haven't even discussed how this will affect the other children," she said, speaking to the others. Though her timing was abrupt (I had an entire agenda planned), she was making a point I hadn't considered. "We raise the children here as equals. Juan will be flying off to the United States and leaving his studies, responsibilities and peers behind. Worse yet, in the U.S., they will spoil him just like the families on the fiesta trips. He will come back with things the other children will never have. I'm afraid it will cause more animosity and problems for him and for everyone."

I had planned to use this meeting to ease the group's mind and reduce resistance to the idea. But once again, I was losing control, and the meeting had just started.

"While this is a major decision, we must realize that if Juan's conditions aren't addressed, they will continue and progress long-term," said Doctor Max, who had softened in his resolve and was inching over to my side of the argument. I knew he wasn't thrilled with this plan, but medically, he knew it might be Juan's only chance at better health and a better life. As the rest of the group considered Doctor Max's comment, he continued. "His open cleft could cause him major problems. Plus, what happens when Juan finally leaves here?"

I chimed in, feeling the need to defend Juan and myself. "You're worried about animosity and problems from the children if he goes to the U.S.? How will the outside world treat him if he doesn't?" I surprised myself with my candor as I addressed Anita directly.

Anita turned to Doctor Max. "Isn't there any way to fix his cleft palate here?" she asked.

"We've discussed this many times, Anita, and every time we evaluate the situation, we come to the same conclusion. It's just too complicated and costly." His tone was soft, almost apologetic. "It's a series of surgeries, each one building on the last. It takes a specialized team."

"And, getting all this care and treatment for free is a great gift," I said, in a soft tone that matched that of Doctor Max. "This is an opportunity that could change his life. If he wants to do it, don't we owe him that?"

"What about his school?" asked Brenda. "What about his two years of service? How will we handle what he is required to give back to NPH?" These were all good questions and valid arguments against the plan. But after an hour of hashing things out, the group agreed that the offer was simply too good to pass up, and they would find a way to deal with any unintended consequences.

"What did Juan say?" Anita asked. "I assume he was in agreement or you would not have asked us back here."

It was easy to ignore her question as they were all talking at once. In reality, I had not heard from Juan since I had proposed the opportunity to him. I was waiting on him and wondering what was going on in his head. I felt getting approval from these folks was the more important starting point, the hard part.

I wanted Juan to come to me as a show of his commitment. I thought if I called him to my office and demanded his decision, he'd decline simply out of spite. On one side, if Juan chose to decline the offer, it would take a load off my mind. I could still say I did everything possible to make it happen. I imagined making the phone call to Father Don in which I told him Juan didn't agree.

On the other side, I imagined the happy ending once the surgeries were complete; the joy for everyone involved, and the gratitude of Juan. My mind swayed back and forth for days.

One of my favorite activities is preparing for weekly Mass. The evening prior was a quiet time in the chapel, cleaning and arranging things. The only sounds were the ones I made. I heard the door at the back of the chapel squeak, and Juan entered. He scooted up the aisle, hopped in the front pew and looked at me.

"Do I have to leave NPH?" he asked.

It was then I realized Juan wasn't afraid of any of it: the

surgeries, the rehab or the travel. He was afraid he'd have to leave his home. Slowly, I walked over and sat in the pew next to him. "No Juan. You will return here after each surgery. It will take a number of procedures to rebuild your mouth and lips, but you will always come back here. NPH will always be your home."

It was one of the core principles of NPH. Our children are not separated from their siblings. They are not put up for adoption. They are secure knowing they will always have NPH as their home even after they leave for adulthood.

He sat quietly.

"Are you afraid of the pain?" I asked.

He shook his head. "I am not afraid of pain. I have felt pain before."

Juan's memory of his burned legs must have been more vivid than I thought. Even at a young age, that kind of trauma was not something easily forgotten.

"I want to be like everyone else," he said flatly, with no fear, no attitude. "Yes, I would like to have the surgery. I want to be proud."

"You should always be proud of who you are, Juan. That pride has more to do with how you treat others and who you are inside than what you look like."

"I want to be proud of how they see me. I want to look good." The slightest smile appeared.

And there it was, his final decision, not for his health or his other issues, but for his looks. I decided right there I would never tell the team that this was a vanity play for him.

At our final meeting, it was my plan to hash out the details. But the tables had turned. The break had allowed each staff member time to reflect and build a list of demands.

Doctor Max began. "If he goes, I must be in communication with his U.S. doctors. They should send complete records of care home with him each time. We must know what is happening so we can provide the follow up care when he returns."

Then it was Brenda's turn. "He must continue his studies. We do him no good if he falls behind and doesn't get an education."

Anita interrupted. "Plus, we have talked it over and all agree, he does not go alone. You must require that a companion accompany him. We can send another boy in his service year to be there for his recovery and to help him through the airports."

I pushed back. "It will add to the cost."

"We will pick someone who has some English skills," Anita continued. "It will protect him, and the two of them can be together if these families do not work out. If they can fly Juan, they can certainly fly another boy, too."

I wanted to protest but I knew they would not hear it. "I'll ask," was all I could say.

"You must not ask, you must tell. It is the only way." Once again, through Anita, the group had gotten the final word. But with any luck, I had secured the path for Juan to get the treatment.

Now I just needed to convince the folks in the U.S. to take two boys instead of one.

#

&

CHAPTER TWELVE

MARLENE DUMPED

I leaned back in the bus seat and exhaled, my first chance to relax since we left Chicago. Coming to El Salvador with two young children was—at best—a leap of faith. Of course, we had traveled before, but suffice it to say, Central America—specifically El Salvador—was never on my bucket list for a family vacation. No matter, I was excited to the see the boys.

Matt hadn't stopped talking about Boris since the NPH fiesta troupe left town, constantly asking questions about the orphanage. Frankly, most of his questions had been swirling around in my own head in recent days and weeks. We'd seen photos on the website but not enough for an understanding of how the kids lived. There was the school and chapel, and photos of happy faces as the kids participated in events or worked on the grounds. But nothing could really paint the full picture. I guess that's true of any place we visit for the first time.

As I looked out the window, the scene looked similar to an hour ago, one small village after another, with stretches of open expanses in between. Were we traveling in circles? Small houses lined the side of the road. Fields set back, some with crops growing in them, others simply large, bare patches of dirt or overgrown with weeds. Another constant was a mountain range in the distance. Since boarding the bus at the hotel, everyone had quieted down. Matt kept his nose pressed against the window. Maggie had fallen asleep on my lap. It was, in a way I can't explain, peaceful, which is odd to say because I still had butterflies in my stomach about the entire situation.

I thought about how different it was compared to my expectations. In my head, I had imagined abject poverty, like the dirty faces you see in those commercials with 800 numbers and websites for donating money. I was fearful of the accommodations, and more importantly, for our safety. I expected the hotel to be different. I'm not sure how exactly, maybe older or smaller, but different. Instead, it was beautiful and modern, a lobby of white couches and granite tile, with large windows that looked out to a huge pool.

And the mountains, always distant but ever present. They were beautiful. I smiled and drew in a deep breath, letting out an equally deep sigh of relief.

Yesterday, when we checked into our room, it was like any other vacation. Matt immediately ran to the large balcony that overlooked the sprawling city of San Salvador to the left and mountains to the right.

"This is awesome!" he shouted as he ran back into the room, jumping on the bed. "Let's check out the TV stations." It amazes me how quickly kids assimilate, and I'm equally amazed by how quickly they can figure out local TV providers.

Brian unfolded the luggage rack and tossed our suitcases on it. "Just remember what we talked about," he said in his most authoritative tone, "You can't drink the water here."

"Not even to brush your teeth," I chimed in. I began digging for the old sock I had packed. In our orientation, they recommended we bring it to put over the faucet head, a constant reminder not to turn on the water. I found it and headed to the bathroom where I realized the hotel had placed rows of bottled water.

"And, you can't put toilet paper in the toilet water like we do at home," said Brian.

"What?" Maggie ran to the bathroom to check out the

situation. Matt was clicking the remote from channel to channel with the volume cranked.

"Where does it go?" Maggie yelled from the other room. We had all been told during orientation, but it didn't really sink in for her until she saw it for herself.

"In the basket on the floor next to the toilet," Brian explained.

"Dirty toilet paper?" she yelled back.

"Yes."

"That's dis*gusting*," she replied. "I'm not putting my paper in that basket." She emerged from the bathroom, shaking her head with her hands on her hips. "No way!" She paused, "Why do they do that?"

I was back in the bedroom unpacking our clothes, but remained silent. I shared her feelings on the issue and had made a personal pact to avoid public toilets at all cost.

"They don't have the plumbing to handle the paper like we do at home," Brian explained.

"I don't care. I am NOT putting my toilet paper in that basket!"

"You have to," Brian said firmly.

"It's all in Spanish," Matt announced from the edge of the bed.

"Of course," remarked Brian. "That's what they speak here."

"Then I'm not wiping," Maggie replied over their conversation.

It was a snapshot moment, the ones you laugh about for the rest of your life. Brian and Maggie arguing about toilet habits, and Matt completely oblivious, cranking the volume, flipping through the channels and wondering why everything was in Spanish, in a Spanish-speaking country. I couldn't help but laugh quietly to myself, thinking, *"Hola!* The Americans have arrived."

On the other hand, I realized the "no flushing your toilet paper" thing would be my issue to face with Maggie in every public bathroom on this trip.

I left my thoughts, returning to the present moment and the quiet of the bus, with Latin music softly flowing through the aisles.

We rode through the Salvadoran countryside in air-conditioned comfort. The only real difference between this ride and one in the U.S. was the police escort that surrounded the three buses. We had been informed that it was for our safety from the *banditos* that prey on and rob rich tourists.

As I looked out the window, I heard Mary Jo talking to Brian. They were discussing the irony of all of us living in the same Chicago neighborhood and never meeting until this trip. "I can't believe we've never met before, at church or the school," she said. "Mel and I have been in the parish forever."

"Were you at the fiesta?" he asked.

"Yes. We hosted the adult chaperones," she answered. I then realized I had seen her name on the list of host families.

"It really wasn't until the kids were at the school that we became more involved," Brian replied. "We got the opportunity to help for the fiesta and learn about NPH. When they planned this trip, we decided it would be a good experience and an opportunity to help out."

I was drawn into the conversation and tried to eavesdrop inconspicuously, but Brian noticed and teased me. "Actually, Marlene decided to come, but got cold feet after they mentioned the armed guards at the informational meeting." He laughed.

I looked at Mary Jo and laughed. "My mother still can't believe I am taking her precious grandchildren to Central America."

As a small town came into view, the bus got very quiet, making the music coming through the speaker seem louder. The bumpy road jostled Maggie awake, and now she was watching the sights on the roadside from my lap. I was captivated by it as well, the beautiful scenery juxtaposed against the small, poor villages, and of course, our security detail. Maggie hadn't said much during the trip (toilet paper conversation notwithstanding). I assumed she was just taking it all in. I was starting to believe this trip was a good idea and would be a great experience for the entire family.

My butterflies were slowly fading.

As we traveled on a steep downhill grade, the scenery

quickly changed. Tin-roofed shacks with open doors and dirt floors now crammed the countryside. I noticed one of the police escorts had begun circling the bus.

"Mom, check out the guards!" Matt yelled putting his face through the crack in the seats in front of Maggie and me.

I looked at Mary Jo and rolled my eyes. "Yes honey. I see them." OK, maybe the butterflies weren't *completely* gone.

"How cool is this? Wait 'til I tell the guys!"

The heavily-armed escorts continued this circling maneuver as the bus made its way through the area. The caravan never stopped, not even for red lights or stop signs. We would see the escort cars pass on the left, slowly moving to the let the buses get ahead again. It was like they were playing leapfrog, I thought, but not like the kind we played when I was a kid in Wisconsin.

Matt chimed in again. "Look at that, Mom! Dad, what kind of guns are those?"

I watched Brian's interest peak as he joined Matt at the window in the row ahead. I wondered why boys loved guns so much. For Brian, working as a police officer, a gun was an everyday thing, part of his uniform for work. "M-16s mostly, and a couple of Uzis," he said without emotion. "Surprising, neither one is very dependable in a firefight."

"Brian! Really?" I reprimanded. He gave me an apologetic look and quietly diverted Matt's attention to the mountains and other "non-lethal" sights and sounds.

As we left the town behind, the scenery changed again. Now, we saw brick and stone houses along the road. In the dirt front yards, children played among chickens and stray dogs. Women hung laundry on clothes lines strung between trees.

"Mom, look! They have pet chickens!" Maggie exclaimed.

"I'm not sure those are pets," Brian replied. Again, I lifted my eyebrows, but this time, he just smiled and winked.

In the distance sat a city of shacks crammed together at the base of what we originally thought was a small mountain. As we approached, the cardboard and metal boxes became visible. So did the massive pile of trash. I noticed dots of color moving on it, at all levels, and we all stared to see what was happening. It became apparent—brutally apparent—this was a village. The children along the road were young, and they stood and stared at our bus as it passed. Their faces were dirty, their clothes torn and ragged. I realized the cardboard and metal configurations were their homes and the "mountain" was a huge garbage dump. The dots were people, rummaging around for anything they could find. This scene of blatant survival will forever be burned in my brain. It was worse than anything I had ever seen on television.

We were all speechless. The butterflies were replaced by a sick pit in my stomach.

"What are those people doing?" Maggie asked. I couldn't answer. I was afraid that if I started talking, I'd break down in tears. This time, Brian's comments rescued me.

"They're garbage picking," he said. Maggie's face showed her disgust.

"Why would they pick through garbage?" Matt asked.

"They're poor, and they're looking for food and clothing." Even Brian, the Chicago cop, was having a hard time explaining it.

Maggie continued. "Who would want to eat someone else's garbage? Why don't they go the store?" People around us smiled, knowing she was innocently asking. In their own minds, they were thinking the same thing. The questions were not rhetorical; Maggie really wanted—needed—to know.

Brian soldiered on. "These people are poor, Sweetheart. They don't have money."

"Well, we should bring them some food," she stated with confidence. A simple answer to such a complicated problem.

"Yes, we should," I answered, then immediately turned my head toward the window.

"Maybe it's like a treasure hunt," Matt added. "There could be cool things thrown away in there."

As the garbage mountain melted away in the distance, the bus remained quiet. The silence was palpable until the bus made a sharp right turn down a dusty, gravel road.

Along the road, the bus passed stone homes that appeared to be small, country farms. Maggie enthusiastically waved out the window at the children running alongside the bus. "Look! They're waving! It must be hot. They don't have shoes on."

Soon, a large stone wall with barbed wire appeared alongside the bus, so close to the road it seemed like if we stuck our hands out the window, we could touch it. Every window was occupied as a large gate came into view. The bus turned slowly and jerked as we pulled over a threshold from the dirt road to a paved driveway. Above us I read, "Welcome to Nuestros Pequeños Hermanos." The convoy pulled slowly into a circle drive, stopping in front of a sprawl of single-story adobe buildings. In the middle of the circle were the children who lived here—476 to be exact—all jumping around, screaming and waving little flags.

Everyone on the bus was frozen, silent. I stared out the window, mesmerized at the surreal scene, a sea of excited children jumping about, laughing and waving for the visitors to come off the bus and join their impromptu celebration. The bus driver stood up and looked down the aisle. He had a puzzled look on his face as we all sat in our seats. I think we were waiting for someone to be the first to stand up. He gestured for all of us to move forward. I imagine he was thinking we were crazy because we came all this way to see this place and then didn't want to get off the bus.

Matt broke the tension for everyone. "There's Boris, Mom!" He charged down the aisle, right past the driver, making us the first ones off the bus. As I stepped down the steps onto the NPH grounds, I didn't see any familiar faces. Then, seemingly out of thin air, Boris and Javier emerged from the crowd. Javier's big smile greeted us, and he immediately wrapped his arms around me. It felt familiar and comfortable.

Boris, however, was standoffish, almost like he had forgotten us. I knew Matt would be crushed. Brian was busy shaking hands with Javier, and Maggie had taken her customary position behind me, peering around my hip. Boris had not moved.

Matt carried a brown paper bag and walked over to Boris. "It's not as big, but it's your wolf." He handed the bag to Boris, who looked confused. But the curiosity was too much for him, so he peeked in the bag. A smile slowly crossed his face as he pulled out the smaller, stuffed Timberwolf. He looked it over and then threw his arms around Matt.

Friends again.

Throughout the day, families spent time with the *pequeños* they had either met at a fiesta or sponsored. The long-term sponsors seemed to share more intimate knowledge than the rest of us. They knew their child's grades and had spent time writing letters as pen pals. Some had visited before. You could see the families sharing photos they had sent over the years.

Mary Jo and I were together at a refreshment bar, grabbing bottled water. She had become friends with the NPH music teacher when they hosted the chaperones on the troupe's trip to Chicago. "We figured the children wouldn't enjoy being with two old people," she laughed, "so we hosted the adults, and it worked perfectly to share wine and food with Otoniel and Maria."

We walked back to find Brian and Mel sitting under a makeshift canopy strung from the trees. The shade was necessary for the Americans, as we all flocked to find relief from the hot sun. Father Ron was standing behind the "gringos," patting them both on the shoulders and laughing. "I'd like to say you get used to the heat, but..." We all laughed at Brian and Mel as they chugged water, their shirts sticking to their bodies.

Matt had joined Boris and other young children in a game of soccer. He was terrible compared to his new friends, but he was having a blast. Maggie was standing on the sidelines watching them and glancing back at us every few minutes. I was proud that she had ventured beyond my immediate perimeter.

"How did you meet Father Don from our parish?" Brian asked Father Ron.

"We worked together in a parish after he returned from Panama. You're both from his parish?"

"Yes, and can you believe that we had to come all the way to El Salvador to meet?" Mel laughed at the irony of it all.

Father Ron looked at Mary Jo. "You mean you didn't know each other at St. Mary's?"

"No," she replied and graciously smiled. "It seems impossible, but we are in different phases of our lives." Again, we all laughed. It felt good to relax and talk about home.

"Did either of you meet a doctor from Shriners at the fiesta?" asked Father Ron as he grabbed the lawn chair I had vacated and sat down. I was surprised he wasn't working the crowd as most leaders do at these types of events.

Mel answered. "Father Don mentioned their charity work at Shriners Hospital."

"Yes, they donate time at Shriners," said Ron. "You see the boy with no legs across the field? His name is Juan Manuel. They want to repair his cleft palate."

"So, they're coming here?" asked Mel.

"No. They want to bring him to Chicago. It will take a series of surgeries to fix the roof of his mouth, his teeth and his lip. I've been told by our people that it's too difficult to handle here."

Brian chimed in, almost under his breath. "What an opportunity."

"Yes, but unfortunately, the idea has met with some... resistance."

"Juan's afraid?" asked Mary Jo.

"No, he's OK with it. The hesitance is mainly with the officials here. They're concerned with how much we'll be doing for a single *pequeño* when there are so many. We like to treat the children equally, and you can understand the possibility for jealousy and resentment. Besides, it's also a logistical issue. You see, we need a place for him to recover in the States after each procedure before we bring him back home."

"Well, if you need a donation..." Mel started.

"That's not the need," Father Ron said. "A group called the Mulliganeers will be covering all the travel. And Shriners is free."

"Then what could possibly be the issue?" Mary Jo asked as she scooched forward in her chair.

At this point, I was preoccupied, watching as Boris tried to get Maggie to join the group on the soccer field. She resisted, but he kept trying.

Father Ron paused, his silence drawing me back into the conversation. "I need some strong advocates in Chicago, families who will take care of Juan while he's there, participate in his care management and communicate back to us."

Father Ron sat back and turned his gaze to the soccer field. "Know anyone?"

Mary Jo chimed in. "Maybe all of us could help." Both Brian and I jerked our heads around. I noticed Mel didn't seem phased at all.

#

♪

CHAPTER THIRTEEN

SAM
COMING TO AMERICA

I wasn't speaking to Juan, just following behind him with the luggage. I tried hard all day not let him see my face when I looked at him, but that wasn't hard. He was busy taking in the attention from the flight attendants, and everyone else. I ignored it. When he acts nice to people, he's very charming, and it makes people want to help him. But as soon as he gets what he wants, he moves on, like he's forgotten someone did him a favor.

I gave him credit, he knew how to play the game, but it upset me every time. Maybe it was just me. Eva seemed to like him. I tried to concentrate on our surroundings because I was afraid of what I might say if I didn't. Olegario had told me I must be helpful and polite for the whole trip. He didn't know my real feelings about Juan. Even Father Ron thought things had gotten better.

After takeoff, when I could open my eyes again, I looked over at him. How could he be so calm? The airplane was bumpy, and it felt like it was about to turn on its side. How could something this big get off the ground? I was sure we were going to crash.

I was holding so tight to the arms of my seat that my knuckles were sore. But not Juan. He was looking out the window, relaxed, enjoying the twists and turns of the takeoff. Every time I looked over at him and saw the ground out the window, I felt my chest tighten. The plane had turned again and it seemed like the ground was coming through the window. I just wanted to be back at NPH, my home.

Beyond my fears of flying, I never wanted any of this. How did I let Olegario talk me into going to Chicago with Juan?

I remembered the day I got called to Olegario's office. Anita, the NPH social worker, told me he wanted to talk. And when Olegario called you to his office "to talk," that was never a good thing. As I washed breakfast dishes that morning, I tried to determine what I had done wrong. Last time, a few of us got caught breaking into the supply shed and stealing food. That was two years ago, but I remember Olegario being so angry. He made me promise not to ever do anything like that again, and I didn't. I wasn't even hanging out with the same guys anymore just to make sure I didn't get in trouble. I liked it here, and I wanted to stay. The thought of being sent back to the old orphanage was always on my mind. Even though Olegario and Father Ron told me that would never happen, that I was part of *la familia* now and would never be sent away, I didn't believe them.

I walked slowly to Olegario's office and sat down in the chair in front of his desk. When he entered, he was smiling, which was strange for him.

"Sam, I have something important to talk to you about," he said. He went on to explain that I had been chosen to go with Juan to the United States, to Chicago, wherever that was. He told me it was a great opportunity. I could practice my English. I could see a new country. I could meet new people and represent NPH.

I sat quietly, respectfully, and listened as it all came rushing at me. When he was done, I sat quietly. After a moment, I said, "I don't want to go."

My comment confused Olegario. I couldn't tell him the real reasons, that I didn't like Juan, I didn't want to leave the only place I ever felt comfortable, and I didn't think I would like any of the people in the U.S. I simply said, "Maybe someone else should go."

Olegario wasn't happy. He told me to think about it and asked me to come back in three days. He wanted me to go to the library and read about Chicago. He told me to have the kids who went to the fiesta tell me their stories.

Eva was the only one I told about the meeting. She loved the idea and started telling me every detail about her time on the fiesta trip. I had to admit her stories about every family and every event made me more interested in going.

Over the next few days, Father Ron had "run into" me several times, and I figured out he was finding me on purpose—in school, on the grounds, as I worked in the cafeteria—to talk me into going with Juan. He sat with me, talking through the details of the trip, the families and the things I would see. When I returned to Olegario's office, I said yes. I knew it would make both Father Ron and Eva happy. And I also realized—not that I cared too much—it would be a good thing to do for Juan.

Now, here I was, on an airplane with Juan, headed to Chicago. I was supposed to be happy, excited even. Lots of other *pequeños* would have been. It was May, and I had just finished high school. But all I could think about was going to a stranger's house, speaking their language, eating their food and waiting on Juan. And, missing Eva. "Someday, I will have control of my own life," I whispered to myself as I tried to push down the fear and anxiety caused by this airplane ride.

I stopped daydreaming when I saw a cart moving down the aisle. What was that for? No one paid any attention to it. Soon, I learned the flight attendants were bringing us food and drinks. I didn't want to spend the money Olegario had given me, so I said no when the flight attendant asked if I wanted anything. Juan took a Coke, and she gave him some snacks, too. She was gone before I realized the drinks were free. Maybe I should have asked him about all this before we got on the plane. He had flown to Chicago before, but I didn't like the idea of him telling me things. He would probably be cocky. He loved it when he knew something someone else didn't. I was thirsty, and it made me wonder if they would come through again and ask if I wanted something.

About four hours into the flight, I heard a "ding" and the pilot came on and said something I didn't exactly understand. The flight attendant came up and down the aisle, looking at our seat belts. I had no idea what it meant but soon found myself grabbing the seat again. The plane was shaking, and I was sure we were in trouble. My stomach was rolling. Juan had fallen asleep and didn't even notice it. How could he sleep through this disaster? I didn't want to die, and I certainly didn't want Juan to be the last person I ever saw. I couldn't tell him how I felt anyway because I didn't want him to see my fear. I kept looking around at the other passengers. No one else seemed scared.

Until I saw the lights of the runway in Chicago, I had no idea if we were crashing or landing. I was so tense, my shoulders hurt. Juan was at the window after his nap, silently watching the whole thing. I was watching too, and I could see lights on the ground, coming closer and closer. They formed perfect squares and seemed to go on forever. I had never seen anything like it. When we hit the ground, I thought the plane would burst.

Juan was busy putting on his legs and getting his crutches from under the seat as the plane drove down the runway. I helped him without saying a word. His legs were heavy and hard to retrieve from under the seat, and his polio crutches were always getting tangled together. At that moment, I felt sympathy for all Juan had to endure. He pulled each leg on under his shorts and then pulled up his sweatpants.

Juan had a small, green bag with strings that went around his shoulders. In it, he was supposed to keep his passport and papers, but I noticed he had crammed these documents in the side pocket of his pants. He was stuffing his green notebook in the bag as people started to get off the plane.

We were in the back of the plane, so I leaned into the aisle and watched what the other passengers were doing as they prepared to get off. Most were getting their luggage down, so I did that and sat back in my seat. I had no idea what to do or where we were going next.

"We will wait for everyone to get off," Juan said as though he'd done this a thousand times.

Finally, it was our turn. We got off the plane and the crew

smiled at Juan as he walked by on his crutches. Outside, a woman in a black vest with a badge around her neck pushed a wheelchair toward us. "Juan?" she asked, but she knew who he was and was speaking to us in Spanish. "I'm Joanna, and I'll take you to customs and baggage claim."

Juan plopped down in the wheelchair and laid his crutches on his lap. I followed as she pushed him up the jetway. I was relieved to be on the ground and happy to hear this woman speak to Juan in Spanish. I could understand everything, and it helped me relax. We were on the way to customs, and I remember Father Ron had told me we would need to show our passports before we went to baggage claim. My job was to take care of the luggage. The slip she held said that there would be a family to meet us. It must be the Byrnes that Olegario and Father Ron had told us about. I hoped they would be there. I hoped they would be nice. I hoped they knew that Juan could be... well, *Juan.*

As we walked through the airport, I noticed so many restaurants, everything from coffee shops, to fast-food places and big areas where people could sit and have a meal. I had never seen anything like it. The airport in El Salvador was much smaller. The smells made me realize I was hungry, but I knew I shouldn't eat. My stomach was making noises from the plane ride. I swallowed hard and hoped things would settle down now that we were safely on the ground.

After customs, Joanna took us to baggage claim. The elevator doors opened slowly, and the only person standing there was a skinny little white boy. He stared straight at us and yelled, "Here they are, Dad!" Then he turned and ran away. It scared me.

Joanna pushed forward, and when we came around the corner, we saw four adults waiting with the little boy. He was talking fast, and I could tell he was excited. Two of the adults looked like they could have been my parents' age. I always wondered what my parents looked like. How did my mom look when she smiled? Did I look like my dad? The other two people were older, like grandparents.

"I recognized them right away, Dad," the little boy said. "That was the elevator I thought they would come down. Their bags should be on Carousel 3." And then, he ran off.

Juan rode in the wheelchair, a single polio crutch sitting on the green backpack on his lap. I had carried the other crutch since it fell off somewhere in the airport. Joanna pushed the wheelchair toward them.

The older woman came to us first. "*Hola*. We are so glad you're here," she said with a smile, which made me feel good. Then, she leaned over to hug Juan. Juan knew them. He had met them at the fiesta and on their visit in El Salvador because they were friends with Otoniel. I had not been to Chicago for the fiesta, so I didn't mix with the visitors when they came to NPH. During the visit, I spent the day in my dorm and only saw the visitors at lunch and when they toured the building.

A tall man walked over and held out his hand to us. "*Hola* Juan. *Hola* Samuel. *Me llamo* Brian."

The older man followed, and after shaking hands with Juan, he grabbed my hand and arm. "How was the flight? I'm Mel." I liked him right away.

"Bumps. I not like it," was all I could say. My stomach was getting worse. The two men laughed.

"Well, it's no wonder. It's windy tonight," said the other woman, the younger one. She seemed to be watching Matt and us very carefully. "I'm Marlene." She shook both our hands and then motioned for us to follow the little boy. "That's Matthew, our son. He's very excited to have you stay with us."

Soon, we were all in a van, riding through the streets. I was sitting in the far back with Matt. He was talking fast, and I was trying to listen while looking out the window. It was dark, yet there were so many people on the streets. At gas stations. Coming out of restaurants. No one seemed scared. Cars were everywhere. This was an even bigger city than San Salvador.

We arrived at the house and headed for the front door. It was a big house with grass and flowers in the yard. A big light lit up the driveway as we unloaded the luggage. I carried Juan's big bag and was setting it down inside the front door when something cold and wet touched the back of my leg. I jumped and screamed. It was the biggest dog I had ever seen. He jumped back too, and Marlene grabbed his collar. "This is Murphy. He's friendly." She was smiling, but I was scared. I reached out to touch the top of his head and his fur was soft on my fingers.

Everyone was coming in the door and talking all at once. But, I couldn't take my eyes off the dog. He was sniffing our legs and then went over to Matt, who hugged his neck.

Soon the older couple said goodbye and left. Until then, I figured they lived here, too.

As Brian showed us the bedroom and bathroom, I kept watching the dog. He sniffed our bags and then walked over to the bathroom, moving between us to get next to Brian. Then, he left the bathroom and headed back toward our bags. I was sure he would bite at something.

I started to notice the room. It was large, and there was a big bed with a headboard against the wall and a smaller mattress in the opposite corner on the floor. Both were made up with nice blankets and pillows. There was a chair in the corner and a dresser against the wall. The bathroom was connected to the bedroom. Could it be just for us? It had a single shower, and there was shampoo and soap on a rack inside with towels folded on the shelf.

Brian was showing us how to turn on the water. I really wasn't listening. He opened a cabinet that had deodorant, shampoo and other bottles lined up. "Just hang them on the towel rack when they are wet," he said. "For the shower, turn the knobs like the sink. It's a good idea to start the water before you get in and wait for it to get warm, and then adjust it to the temperature you want." I couldn't understand all of what he was saying, so I just smiled and nodded.

As Brian started to leave with Matt, he turned and said, "Oh yeah, remember that here in the States you can put your toilet paper in the toilet. Okay?"

That I understood. Father Ron had told us. As he left, I turned around and there was Murphy sitting down next to our bags. I wasn't sure what to do. I looked at Juan. He had already plopped down on the big bed. "This one is mine, you take the one on the floor," he said.

I wasn't about to argue, so I just nodded. Besides, I couldn't stop staring at that huge dog, which had walked over to lie on my bed on the floor. "What should I do?" I asked Juan.

"Come here, boy!" Juan said, and Murphy went right to him. Juan put his face on Murphy's head like they were old friends. I was frozen, and all I could think was, "Are you crazy? This beast is going to bite your head off!"

"Murphy!" The call came from downstairs. The dog jumped up and headed toward the voice. "Is he up there?" Marlene asked.

"Yes," Juan answered and started laughing. He immediately relaxed back on the big pillows against the headboard and opened his green notebook. One thing that amazed me about Juan was his ability to get comfortable in any situation. I envied that, but I also knew envy was a sin, so I tried to put it out of my mind. I began to unpack. I put my folded clothes in piles on top of my suitcase. I set my extra shoes in line with the wall. I took my toothbrush and paste to the bathroom and put them on the counter.

That night, I lay awake, wishing I could talk to Eva. I missed home. Home? I never thought I would call NPH home. I remember when I first arrived, and how Father Ron tried for so long to get me to talk to him. It seemed so long ago. I didn't like him then. But now, thinking about NPH and Father Ron made me smile. He was my friend, someone I trusted. I knew he thought this was an opportunity for me, something that would help me as well as Juan. But at that moment, as I lay in a strange bed, in a strange house, in a strange land, it didn't feel that way. I sat up and went to the window. We were on the second floor of the house, and I could see rooftops. It was bright on the street, large lights shining on the blacktop. Even the sky looked brighter than back home. I pushed the curtain open and went back to lay down, staring out at the sky, the same sky that hung above NPH, but different in so many ways. I wondered what everyone was doing back there.

In the morning, Juan was asleep, but I had been awake for over an hour. I was so hungry. I realized I hadn't eaten anything since we left home. Marlene offered us food last night, but when I looked at those sandwiches, I realized my stomach was still hurting from the flight and I couldn't eat. I could smell food cooking and decided I didn't want to wait for Juan. I got dressed and went down the stairs. Marlene was at the stove, and I sat on a chair at the counter.

I didn't think she heard me enter the kitchen and was surprised when she said, "Good morning, Samuel," as she kept working. Without turning around, she asked "Are you hungry?"

"Yes," I said, and she set down a plate of eggs, sausages and toast. I ate everything. Marlene asked me a few question that I politely answered. I noticed Matt and Maggie watching TV. They came to the kitchen to eat too, and as soon as I finished, I put my plate by the sink and headed back upstairs. They seemed nice, but I didn't know what else to do.

CHAPTER FOURTEEN

MARLENE
THE CARDS FALL INTO PLACE

I was staring at a tiny crack forming on our bedroom ceiling. I couldn't sleep. I had so much going through my head. Juan and Sammy had returned two days ago for their second visit. In one respect, having gone through this once before made things easier. Logistically, we knew what to expect, and had the general process down pat. But this time, the stakes were much higher, much more buttoned down, and for good reason. This time, there would be few—if any—games or funny movies or long talks over coffee. This visit was a business trip, filled with tests, x-rays and appointments, culminating in Juan's first surgery. Mary Jo and Mel had already taken Juan to his intake appointment. Tomorrow, we would meet the surgeons at Shriners.

"The doctors said they will provide a full list of post-op instructions, so we know just what to do once he comes home," Mary Jo told me over the phone. It was during that conversation I realized how important she was for me, and on a larger scale, to this entire process. She had so much enthusiasm and always seemed confident we were doing the right thing.

I was scared. I wasn't a nurse. In fact, I hated blood and never considered nursing or any career in medicine. What was I thinking by taking this on? How would I be able to handle Juan after his surgery? How would I deal with his recovery, especially if it didn't go according to plan? (I love plans but only when they work.)

I ran through the reunion in my head. The boys had been quiet this time. Very quiet. Frighteningly quiet. After we brought them home, I made sandwiches, called them to the kitchen and waited, ready to talk about our schedule. Or about anything, really. After a while Sam came downstairs and asked if he could take his sandwich up to the room. They were obviously hunkered down in the upstairs bedroom. I agreed. Then he came back down to ask if he could bring Juan's upstairs as well. I nodded and sat alone in the kitchen. Alone with my thoughts and my fears.

I kept myself busy with everyday chores (mostly just to pass the time and keep my mind from wandering to the "worst-case scenario"), Juan entered the room without his legs. It startled me. I don't know why it still surprised me when I saw him like that. I tried not to show it, but it was still shocking. Juan's upper body was strong and wide but without his prosthetics, it looked almost like he had fallen through the floor up to his hips. The realization of how high up his legs were amputated made me wonder about the fire and how he could have survived.

I told myself to stop obsessing, rolled over in bed and plumped my pillow to try a new position in an attempt to doze off for a few hours before the alarm went off. But then, my thoughts ran to Matt and Maggie. How were they interpreting these visitors? I had hoped their interaction would be like it was with Boris and Javier, but it wasn't. How could it be? These boys were older. They didn't talk much to each other. They knew less English than Javier. This time, it seemed like we were simply boarding a couple of strangers, not really interacting, and I wondered what that meant for my kids.

After we picked them up from the airport, Juan and Sam went out to eat with Mel and Mary Jo. I made dinner and took the opportunity to talk to Matt and Maggie about the boys. At seven years old, Maggie didn't say much, just a few questions about Juan's legs. Matt seemed disinterested. "I don't know, Mom. They seem fine." He shrugged off my questions and started asking about his baseball team and when practice would start. Summer was here, and he loved being with his friends.

I rolled over again, punching the pillow. How would we manage after the surgeries? If the boys never engaged with us, could we really care for Juan? Would we be able to talk with him if something was wrong? Would Juan open up if he was in pain?

I don't know when I finally drifted off to sleep, but before I knew it, morning had come and my body felt like it was filled with lead. I turned off the alarm and headed to the kitchen to make coffee. At least we had this in common. Both Sam and Juan loved coffee. I knocked on their door to get them both moving.

Sam appeared in the kitchen first. His hair was wet, and he was dressed in a nice shirt and pants, ready to go.

"Coffee?" I asked.

"Yes," he smiled. As I poured a cup for him, he asked, "Sugar?"

I brought down the sugar bowl and watched as he spooned teaspoon after teaspoon in his cup. He must have caught me staring. "I like sugar," he said. He was embarrassed. I laughed to lighten the mood.

Sam and I both had toast, and I went to finish getting ready. Back in the kitchen, I kept looking at my watch. If Juan didn't come down soon, he wouldn't get any breakfast. Finally, I said to Sam, "Where is Juan?"

Sam jumped off the stool at the counter, "I get him." He practically ran out of the kitchen, and I hoped my tone hadn't been too cross.

I checked outside. Mel and Mary Jo were already in the driveway. They offered to drive us all to the appointment. When Juan and Sam finally came downstairs, I grabbed my purse and started for the door. Juan sat down at the counter as if we had time to eat. I said, "I'm sorry Juan but we have to go. We can't be late to the doctor, and Mary Jo and Mel are outside." He seemed mad but got his crutches and stood to leave.

Juan got in the backseat and handed his crutches to Sam, who put them in the trunk. Sam and I settled in the back as well. "Good morning. We brought you coffee," Mary Jo said with a smile.

"Thank you," I said. "You always know what we need."

"I don't want coffee," Juan said in an angry monotone. This silenced the group and changed the entire vibe in the car.

"Well, that's okay," Mary Jo continued in her perky style. "I can always drink two."

She pulled out a paper and began to read it to us. "Today, we will see both Doctor Reisberg and Doctor Patel at their offices at UIC Medical Center. This is the final evaluation before the surgery."

"Are their offices close to one another?" I asked.

"We have only been to Doctor Reisberg's so far, so I am not sure," Mary Jo answered.

"I would assume they're both in the craniofacial unit," Mel added.

When we pulled up to the building, Mel pulled under the portico to drop us off. It took some time for Juan to swing his prosthetic legs out of the car, bring himself to a standing position and secure his crutches. The anxiety of the visit and my impatient personality made me realize his slow movements were starting to drive me crazy. "It must be difficult to always need so much extra time," I thought, resisting the urge to step in and help.

The examination room was small, not because it was any different than any other but because we had five nervous people jammed into it, and the doctor hadn't even arrived. Mary Jo was making small talk about the "wonderful things that were going to happen." Sam stood in the corner like a soldier, and I nodded my head and smiled, pretending to agree with her. Juan sat with his head down, disinterested. I wondered if he really understood what was about to happen. Wasn't he scared?

The door burst open, and Doctor David Reisberg appeared, outwardly happy to see Mary Jo and Mel again. They introduced me, and then he got right to work.

Doctor Reisberg was Director the University of

Illinois-Chicago Craniofacial Center and Head of Maxillofacial Prosthetics. He would work with Doctor Pravin Patel, the Craniofacial and Pediatric Plastic Surgeon who also donated time to Shriners Hospital in the repair of Juan's cleft palate and the replacement of his mangled teeth.

As Doctor Reisberg examined Juan's mouth, he told us a story.

"It's amazing how all this is coming together," he started. "I golfed last summer at an outing for UIC. On the course, I met a man who was involved with an organization called the Mulliganeers. He told me about their mission to help families who needed money for healthcare or other issues involving their children. He told me to keep his card and call him if I ever needed anything."

He was now examining Juan's ears, but never stopped talking.

"So that card sat on my desk for over a year until Pravin talked to me about this case. We knew it would be a drain for the orphanage to pay for Juan's airfare back and forth for these surgeries."

He was feeling Juan's neck.

"Right after Pravin and I talked about this case, I was sitting at my desk looking at the files and noticed that card sticking out from under my pile of stuff." He laughed and shook his head. "I couldn't believe it when I called. Jack—the contact name on the card—listened to Juan's story and called me back the next day to say they would pay for whatever flights were necessary to make this happen."

Now he looked Juan right in the eye. "You have someone looking out for you upstairs," he said. His nurse repeated everything in Spanish.

Juan looked at him and then the ceiling. He obviously didn't know what "upstairs" meant. Doctor Reisberg looked up, realized and laughed.

"I don't mean up there," he said. "I mean *way* up there. God is looking out for you." Juan smiled as it was translated.

It was the first time I'd seen Juan smile, and it was the first time I felt like things might be OK. But it was also the first time I noticed the terrible condition of Juan's teeth.

The important thing—and something that eased my mind—was that Juan seemed to like Doctor Reisberg. It wasn't at all surprising. If you met him, you'd immediately understand why we all liked him.

After the next appointment, with Doctor Patel, we stopped for lunch at a nearby Mexican restaurant, and the mood had lightened considerably.

"I think these doctors are saints," Mary Jo said. "The fact that they donate their talent to kids like Juan, it's fabulous, just incredible."

"I have to agree." I chimed in, feeling a sense relief. "Doctor Reisberg is so confident in his team, it feels like we are doing the right thing."

As we continued talking, we realized Juan and Sam were laughing. Not just a little giggle but belly laughing so hard Sam was almost on the floor. "What are you two doing?" Mel asked.

"Tasting hot," Sam said as he fanned his hand in front of his mouth with one hand and pointed at the hot sauce he'd tried. He was sweating and laughing so hard it was infectious. Soon, we were all laughing.

Juan, too, was in obvious discomfort from the hot sauce. He was wiping tears from his eye and laughing at the same time.

"We see who can eat more," Sam explained. "Nobody leave these on tables in El Salvador." The two boys had started a contest to try all the hot sauces at the restaurant. Sammy continued to laugh as he told us Juan was losing. From our vantage point, it looked like a tie.

#

$\text{\textit{\&}}$

CHAPTER FIFTEEN

SAMUEL
ROOM 122

It was cold outside, colder than anything we could imagine in El Salvador. I didn't like the cold, but seeing my breath in the air was cool. I was tired too, because we had left the house early. We arrived two days ago, and now we were at the hospital for the big surgery.

As I walked through the sliding doors, I smashed both sides of the door frame with Juan's crutches. I was carrying them and following behind as he was being pushed in a wheelchair. I guess I was distracted, looking around at what was supposed to be a hospital, but it didn't look like any hospital I ever saw. The lobby had beautiful couches, carpeting with crazy, colorful designs. There were toys, books and a tree with photos clipped to the branches. I could see the pictures of children with staff members, and they were all smiling.

I followed the rest of the group as we walked up to the front desk. The sign above it said, "Welcome to Shriner's Hospital." It was early morning and the lobby was empty, but you could almost feel the energy of the building. Soon this place would be filled with children and buzzing with activity.

An old man walked toward us. He was wearing a red box on his head with a tassel sticking out of it. I moved behind Brian.

"I'm Robert," he said, smiling as he extended a hand. "And

who is this?" Right away, he focused on Juan. I looked at Juan. I could tell he was tired and probably nervous, but his expression was like it always was; basically, non-existent. That was my cue, and as I often did, I spoke for Juan. "This is Juan Manuel Pineda."

Juan followed up with, "Hello."

"Well, welcome to Shriners. I will be your guide and take you to Juan's room," Robert said. He turned and signaled for us to follow him to the check-in desk. I still wondered about that funny hat. Was that so we wouldn't lose him on the trip to Juan's room? Later, I saw others wearing them, so I stopped trying to figure it out, and decided maybe I'd ask Brian later on.

We checked in and followed Robert through an open hallway. Everything at Shriners was big and open. And it felt different. Other hospitals smelled like sanitizers. This place was more like a hotel.

Robert walked us to a balcony railing that overlooked a large area with a basketball court, ping pong tables, playground equipment and a game room. "This is where the kids come to have some fun when they are recovering and starting to feel better," he explained.

The area had two-story windows and large doors that opened to an outdoor area just as big and bright as this one. It was late November. Many leaves had fallen on the ground, and it looked perfect for playing outside. The leaves left on the trees and shrubs were colorful and the grass was perfectly manicured. Again, you could almost feel the activity and energy of this place, even though at that moment, it was completely empty and quiet.

"Juan and the whole family can use anything in the place," Robert said. He turned to two nurses who joked with him and said hello to us. "The cafeteria is just down that hall and remember everything, even for the family, is free." Robert walked a step ahead of us but kept talking to us over his shoulder. He was very friendly.

"Here we are, Room 122," he said. "I will leave you now, but please stop any of us if you need any help while you are here." OK, maybe that's why they were wearing the funny hats, so they'd be easy to find if we had any questions.

Juan's room was like being in a hotel. It had two beds, a closet for his things, a chair and a big television. Luckily for us, there was no roommate this morning so we could use the whole space. After a moment or two, I started putting away Juan's things.

I decided if I ever needed medical care, I would want it at a place like this. I could hear the nurses walking by. Everyone said hi, and they all knew the patients' names. I would learn later that "Shriners" is not just a place, but a group of people dedicated to caring for the less fortunate, especially children who suffer from burns and terrible diseases. They donate their money and volunteer time so they can give children care when no one else will. It made me think of Father Wasson, the priest who founded NPH. These people were like him.

Suddenly, a doctor entered the room. He moved quickly and talked even faster. "Good morning," he said with a smile. "I am Doctor Patel." He immediately went to Juan, which I liked. Sometimes, it felt like Marlene and Brian or Mel and Mary Jo were talking around us instead of directly to Juan. But Doctor Patel was different. His focus was on Juan and it made both of us happy. Behind him was a beautiful nurse. She was young and Latina. I stood up a little taller. "Margarita is here to help translate if there are any questions."

"*Hola*, Juan," Margarita said, and then smiled and nodded at me.

Doctor Patel grabbed a chair and dragged it across the room to where Juan was sitting as he talked. "I will be Juan's doctor along with David Reisberg."

Mary Jo chimed in. "We met you at his intake appointment. We are his host family."

"Good. You'll be a very important part of his recovery," he said has he shook her hand and continued across the room toward Juan.

He placed the chair close to Juan and sat down face to face with him. As he began explaining the steps to fixing Juan's face, I was impressed with his explanation. He gave a lot of details, but it was simple so even I could understand him without Margarita explaining it in Spanish. Doctor Patel never took his eyes off Juan. We all just listened. Even Mary Jo and Marlene, who usually had lots of questions, remained quiet.

Doctor Patel could do a lot of things at once but still make the person he was talking to seem like the only thing on his mind. I noticed nurses lining up outside the door, waiting for him with charts for other patients.

Father Ron had told me Juan's first procedure in this two-year journey would involve taking bone from his hip and using it to rebuild his upper mouth. That's what Doctor Patel was explaining to Juan. He talked about the procedure, the incision and the recovery. It all sounded awful to me. I was glad I was not Juan.

After Doctor Patel left, Margarita took over, re-explaining everything in both English and Spanish. She told Marlene and Mary Jo that the host family would need to bring Juan dinner every evening from the cafeteria, wash his bedding and clothes, and be there for his recovery. "Maybe this place isn't so great after all," I thought. Why didn't they bring in his food? Is this how all U.S. hospitals operate?

I never realized how boring this trip would be. Our first day, we waited more than four hours before Juan came out of surgery. The chairs in the waiting room were stiff, and all we could do was watch TV. After a while, I decided to walk around the hospital. One room had a ping pong table, so I went in and looked around. But then, a family entered, and I left.

Everything went OK, according to Doctor Patel, and he seemed excited when he came into the waiting room. He went over the procedure with Mary Jo and Marlene, and explained Juan's recovery. Then he was gone again. A nurse was chasing after him down the hallway as he left.

We waited for Juan to return to his room. Marlene told me he had to stay in the recovery area until they thought he was stable enough to be in his room. It seemed like a long wait, but at least we had time to get something to eat.

When they brought Juan back, he was miserable and in pain. His whole face was swollen and red. Talking hurt him, so he just nodded or shook his head to answer questions. There were ice packs on both sides of his face. I imagined they were helpful, but not very comfortable. Mary Jo did most of the talking. Marlene held his hand and looked like she was going to cry.

A nurse came in and gave us a final update on what would happen. She said we should go home and come back the next day. They said if anything happened, they would call Marlene and Mary Jo.

Each day was the same. I would go to the hospital with Mel and Mary Jo and spend the morning sitting in Juan's room. In the afternoon, I'd go to Marlene's house and watch Spanish television. Then, in the evening, I'd return to the hospital with Brian or Marlene.

One evening, I was with Marlene and when we entered Juan's hospital room, he had a roommate. It was an older boy, about Juan's age, who seemed to have the same swollen face from a cleft palate. He was lying back in his bed watching a Spanish television show with Juan.

I noticed a woman sitting on the chair. Marlene entered and introduced herself. The woman wore a long gown with a white bonnet. Marlene was dressed in a business suit. They looked very different.

The woman explained she and her son had traveled from Pennsylvania. Marlene tried to explain her role in Juan's life. It was a long conversation. I offered to go and get Juan's dinner from the cafeteria.

When I returned, Marlene asked me to carry a laundry basket and follow her and the roommate's mother. We entered a small laundry room down the hall from Juan's room. Marlene started to explain the wash machine to the woman.

"You put the clothes in here, along with some detergent—the soap—and press this button," she explained.

"How does it work?" the woman asked as she looked down into the hole.

"Well, water comes in and splashes around with the soap to clean the clothes." The woman looked at her, confused. Marlene continued. "Then, it spins out the water and fills again to rinse out the soap. At the end, it spins so the clothes are just damp."

"Then what do I do?" the woman asked.

Marlene moved to the dryer, opened it and continued. "The clothes go in here, and hot air blows as the clothes roll around until they're dry."

As we were leaving, I saw Marlene lean into Juan and whisper. "Put on an English-speaking station so Ryan can watch TV, too."

In the car, Marlene tried to explain that the family was Amish. They don't have access to hospitals, but her son was so ill they decided to get him treatment and came to Shriners. The woman did not have electricity and had never used a washing machine or dryer. Her religious beliefs were about living a simple life. And I thought we lived simply in El Salvador.

"Can you imagine, she has eight children and washes all those clothes by hand?" Marlene said. "She'll probably go home and tell her husband to go get her a wash machine."

"Why does she wear the bonnet?" I asked.

"I don't know exactly, but I believe it is part of the culture for Amish woman or girls. They don't use electricity. Can you imagine not being able to watch TV?"

"Why?" I asked.

"It's just part of their belief system. They believe in living simply. No electricity, no television, no cars, and I think they basically live off of what they grow and raise on their farms."

"Is that why you told Juan to change the channel?" I realized.

"Yes, that poor boy can't use the remote control, so I thought putting on an English-speaking station was the least we could do for him. Maybe it will make his recovery easier."

"It's either that or he'll go home to all his friends and tell them they're not missing anything because TV is all in Spanish." I had to laugh.

#

𝄞

CHAPTER SIXTEEN

FATHER RON
HARD ROAD

I was walking out of the sacristy when my phone rang. On and off all week, I had been thinking about Juan. Initially, I hoped my trip coinciding with his surgery would afford me time to participate in this first procedure, but I had been called by the Bishop to officiate a funeral, so I missed it. With Juan on my mind, I had included his story in my homily.

"A Life Well Lived" was the theme Jack's family requested, and it was printed on the funeral flyer they had provided to the mourners. His family told me Jack never wanted pity, and they couldn't see celebrating the end of his life with any either. Jack's life had been filled with love, and the people who showed up to celebrate his life reflected that fact.

My phone rang. It was Mel.

"How is he?" I asked anxiously, wishing my schedule would have allowed me to do the funeral and still be on hand for Juan's surgery.

"He's in recovery, and Doctor Patel thinks it went well," Mel explained.

"Wonderful!"

Mel continued. "They took a piece of bone from his hip. The

doctor said it may complicate his mobility with the prosthetics, but otherwise all went as expected." What a relief it was to know things had gone according to plan.

"Let him know we will be there throughout his recovery," I heard Mary Jo chime in from the background.

"Mary Jo wants me to tell you...

"Tell her I'm grateful. I'll plan a visit tomorrow."

As I hung up, I saw a young man waiting for me outside the church. He looked weary and nervous. I recognized the signs. He needed my help. I forgot about Juan and turned my focus to the man in need.

The next day, I visited Shriners. It was early and Juan was alone in his room, covered with a blanket up to his chin.

As I entered, he turned to reveal his face, swollen and red, and it reminded me once again how difficult this journey would be for him. I smiled and pulled a chair next to his bed.

Facing difficult moments is part of my job as a priest. I learned early on to remain calm in such situations, and often, silence is better than small talk or encouragement.

"Good morning," I said as I rested my hand on his forearm. He looked up at me, and then slowly closed his eyes. This was one of those times when silence would provide the best counsel.

Before I left, I prayed with him. For courage. For strength. For healing. I noticed his hands, now on top of the covers, squeezed tightly in prayer.

Once back in the car, I prayed again.

Dear God,
Give Juan strength as he recovers
from this difficult surgery.
Be with him, and
give him the strength
to face each challenge.
Help his body heal quickly.
Bless all those who care for him,

> at the hospital and at home.
> Bless them and give them patience.
> Amen.

How could life seem so easy for some and so incredibly difficult for others? It was one of the many questions I routinely asked God.

Two weeks later, I visited the Byrnes. I was excited to see Juan after reports that his healing was going well. I expected a much better visit and conversation now that he had some time to recover.

Matt answered the door with Murphy at his side. Luckily, I had already met Murphy and knew he was a calm and friendly dog, although his size could be intimidating. "Mom, it's Father Ron," Matt yelled.

As I came in the door, Marlene greeted me with a dish towel swung over her shoulder. "Father, it's great to see you!" She walked me through the kitchen and into the family room, where Juan was on the couch, wrapped in a blue, fuzzy blanket. His face was more swollen than I expected, and it was purple with bruising. On the coffee table sat crushed tissues next to a glass of water, along with a half-dozen bottles of prescription medications lined up in a row. A piece of paper had a handwritten chart to track times for Juan's medicines.

"How are you feeling?" I asked as I sat next to him.

"Not too good," he answered, but didn't sit up.

From behind me, Marlene added, "The recovery is rough. Both the incision on his hip and his face hurt quite a bit. But the doctors told us this is normal."

I had forgotten about the second incision on his hip. It meant he couldn't use his prosthetics for the foreseeable future.

"Juan, I am sorry it is taking such a long time to heal," I said.

He closed his eyes and said nothing. His demeanor spoke volumes.

"Does the pain medicine help you?" I asked.

He opened his eyes and shrugged, "Some."

"Can you sleep?"

"Some."

"That's good. Each day should get better," I said.

"Maybe, but not so far," he replied quietly. He was down, really down. This wasn't the Juan I had come to know.

"Are you doing everything the doctor says?" I asked.

"Yes."

Marlene, now back in the kitchen but overhearing our discussion, broke in. "He doesn't rinse his mouth enough." I could hear her frustration.

"It enough," Juan replied quietly so she couldn't hear him. It made me laugh, but I could tell tensions were running high for everyone.

I grabbed the chart and looked at the columns. I could see empty squares under the "Rinse Mouth" column. The chart had day after day of doses, topical applications, mouth rinsing and bandage changes followed by notes. It was then I realized the magnitude of Juan's recovery and the amount of work he and all his caregivers had to put in to ensure a good outcome.

In the car on the way home I was feeling down, like my visit did nothing to help any of them.

Dear God,
Help Juan heal and take away his pain.
Give strength to Brian and Marlene, Mel and Mary Jo.
Bless them for their caring,
I ask you to walk with Juan on this journey.
Lift his spirits.
Give him courage, and
help his body heal.
Amen.

As I drove, I reminded myself that time heals. I convinced myself that this was just a bad day for Juan and Marlene, and it would pass. Next time would be different.

#

♪

CHAPTER SEVENTEEN

MARLENE
AN EASTER WAVE

I was sitting on the beach, the sun warming my skin, waves crashing in front of me, feeling guilty, happy and conflicted all at the same time. It's always wonderful to see Brian's father for any holiday and this year, it was Easter. He had moved to Florida full-time after "Grandmama" passed away (that's what the kids called her), leaving Brian's family home in Chicago. As Brian tells it, "One morning, Dad made a cup of tea, stirred it with the spoon, took a last sip and left for the airport saying 'today is the day,' and that was that. He was gone to Florida to start a new life."

"Good for him," I thought at the time. His strength and faith would carry him on without her.

The spoon was still sitting on the counter when Brian and his siblings began cleaning out their childhood home. That was years ago, and now, his Florida condo had turned into the winter getaway for all the Byrne siblings and their families. And it didn't take long for all of us to realize that Brian's dad was "home," only with much better weather.

We loved coming to see him. Each of Brian's siblings took turns visiting him over the major holidays. He never asked us to, and never would have put pressure on any of us, but we knew he wouldn't want to burden his neighbors during their holiday celebrations. They would have invited him, and he would have fought them because he hated the idea of imposing on anyone.

This year, Easter was our turn to visit, and as always, it was great to see him and to get away.

That said, I felt guilty, and I knew why. Juan was back in Chicago in the hospital, and I wasn't there for him. As I sat on the beach, I went back and forth in my mind, between the guilt I felt and asking myself, "How had I become so deeply entrenched in this kid's health, and his life? When had he become just a normal part of my day?"

As I dug my feet in the sand, I didn't come up with any answers, but one thing was for sure: Juan and Sam had become an integral part of our family. The coordination of their flights, appointments, school and daily routines had become as ordinary as packing lunches for the kids or watching Brian head off to work.

And three days before our Florida trip, I realized just how much. I was alone at the airport, waiting at the Starbucks near baggage claim for the boys to arrive. What once was a group greeting, a big deal, was now a normal occurrence. It was just me. In fact, Sam found me before I saw him. That's how "regular" the scene had become.

Juan seemed unsettled when we checked him in at Shriners the next day. "Why are you going to Florida?" he asked. I tried to assure him that I would stop in the next morning before his procedure, and that we would be back soon so we could be with him for part of his recovery before he returned to NPH. He didn't like that answer and remained more agitated than normal.

The next morning, I picked up Mary Jo and Mel early, so we had plenty of time to get to Shriners and see Juan before they took him to surgery. When we arrived, he was a sight to see, sitting straight up in bed, legs off and draped in a long hospital gown. For most patients, these gowns are short, but for Juan it hung two feet below his stumps. He was always getting tangled in the extra fabric.

Doctor Patel did a typical pre-surgery visit with Juan, and we listened. He always brought a bilingual nurse with him, explaining everything in English before the nurse explained it again in Spanish. Even if Juan understood most of what he heard in English, Doctor Patel insisted all conversations be given in both languages to make sure no detail was missed.

As Doctor Patel spoke, Juan kept his eyes on me. When he was done, Juan simply said, "Marlene won't be here."

Doctor Patel smiled. He knew about our Florida plans. "Juan, Mel and Mary Jo have you covered. Compared to the last few surgeries, this is an easy one. Don't worry."

I couldn't decide why Juan was worried about us going away. Was it his recovery? Was it a security thing? Was he worrying about staying with Mel and Mary Jo?

I stayed until they wheeled him to surgery. He was quiet but hugged me before I headed home to finish packing. The kids were off school and had been delighted to sleep in.

In a few hours, we packed our bags and were on our way back to Shriners for a last visit before we left. I remembered Juan's eyes when he woke up. He seemed surprised I was there, even though we had told him many times we would stop on our way to the airport. Sam had come with us too. He would stay with Juan until Mel and Mary Jo's visit in the afternoon, then return to their house for the week. He had a small drawstring bag of things to take to their house.

"Are you sure you don't need more clothes for the week?" I had asked him as we left the house.

"No, this is enough," Sam said. I laughed at the thought of the luggage we had packed for our Florida trip compared to his tiny bag.

I was jarred from my thoughts when I heard Maggie yelling, "Mom! Come in the water!" I waved from the sand. I love to swim but hate the salty taste of the ocean. So, I waded in up to my waist and watched Matt, Brian and Maggie jump over the waves. The weather in Florida was heavenly compared to the winter we were facing in Chicago. I understood why Grandmama and Grandad loved escaping here every winter, and why now, Grandad has chosen to make this his permanent home.

After the beach, we got dressed and went into town for some Easter shopping. Once the groceries were unpacked, we went for a swim in the pool. The kids couldn't get enough swimming, whether it was open water or in a pool. For me, there was nothing like the clear water of the pool. I loved it and also figured it cleaned all the salt off my family. Grandad came and sat poolside to watch us. All of us wearing swimsuits in the sun and him in a sweater and boots. He was always cold.

I decided to call Mel and Mary Jo to see how things were going, even though I already knew Juan's surgery had gone fine, and he wouldn't be released for two more days. Doctor Patel had predicted this recovery would be easier than the last, but I wanted to check in. Calling to wish them Happy Easter was the perfect excuse.

"Happy Easter. How are you?" I was glad Mary Jo answered the phone. You always get more details than if you talk to the men.

"We are great. How is Florida?" she answered.

"Fantastic. Brian's dad is doing great. The weather is gorgeous. I understand why people move here in the winter. We enjoyed a day at the beach, with stops at the pool."

"That sounds perfect!" she replied.

"How is your Easter? Have you seen Juan?" I asked.

"Actually, we went to visit him but left before he saw us."

"Is something wrong?"

"No. I believe today was what I call an Easter miracle," she said. "Mel, Sam and I went over early this morning to see him. We wanted to attend Easter Mass at the hospital. When we got there, we heard guitar music coming from his room."

"Who was visiting?"

"It wasn't a visitor," she continued. "A young intern who had assisted Doctor Patel in surgery was with Juan when we arrived. He found out Juan liked to play music and was in the room playing guitar with him."

"What do you mean *with* him? Juan can play guitar?" I was stunned.

"Not only can he play guitar, this young doctor brought two, and they were playing together. It was the most beautiful thing I have heard in a long time."

"Really?"

"Yes, Juan is very good. The three of us just stood against the wall and listened, but we didn't interrupt. We decided to leave them in the moment." I could hear the smile in her voice.

"That's amazing," I replied. "What a surprise. I wonder how the doctor discovered he could play."

"I wish you could have heard it, Marlene. It was so peaceful and comforting."

I knew how much Mary Jo loved music and the arts in general. She and Mel were always attending a symphony, concert or play. Her appreciation was deep.

We talked for a while longer, and when I hung up, I wished I could have heard Juan play. I recalled all the time he'd spent at our computer, searching for songs and downloading music. It somehow made more sense now.

#

𝄞

CHAPTER EIGHTEEN

SAM
DRIVING AROUND WITH FATHER RON

Even though it was hot, I had the windows closed. The music was blaring, and I was drumming my thumbs on the steering wheel. I kept an eye out for Father Ron, so I could turn the radio off before he opened the passenger door.

It had been a great week. Eva and I were sneaking away and talking every chance we could. She wanted to know everything about my time in Chicago. What we ate. Where we slept. What the snow was like.

She was very happy about the idea of me attending English school. I told her about speaking to the family in their language. I think it made them happy. I talked about how we watched this funny show where people did stupid things on video and then sent in the footage. I told her about Maggie. She teased me because she predicted I would learn to like traveling to the U.S. and that I might even learn to like the family. She loved children and said she would like to meet all of them, especially Maggie.

One night, I even confessed how I felt about Juan. I explained how he had taken the big bed, how he left his dishes for me to pick up and many of the other things he did.

"Is that why you were mad at me after the fiesta, because I was being nice to him?" she asked.

I had to confess I was jealous.

She laughed out loud. "I don't give my heart away that easily!"

I liked her pride, but even more, I loved the way she smiled at me. She had a way of showing her admiration, and it made me dream of bigger things for the future. She wanted things too, like to go to nursing school. She hoped to care for sick children.

"I think you should study hard at English," she said. "If you can speak both languages, it will be good for your future."

I wasn't sure how it could help me. At NPH, no one ever spoke English except the guests who visited. I nodded like I thought it was a good idea. Almost anything she said sounded good.

I was still daydreaming and got startled when Father Ron yanked open the passenger door. I quickly reached to turn off the radio.

"Whoa. That is some song," he said with a laugh. "You don't have to turn it off, but maybe just not quite so loud."

That day, we were going to Santa Ana, where Father Ron had several meetings. While he was working, I'd walk around and maybe find some lunch. We talked a lot during the trip. Father Ron loved conversation.

"Tell me more about your trip," he said. "In English."

"It good," I replied with a smile.

"I understand Marlene enrolled you in English school. How is that going?"

Two days ago, my answer may have been different, but now that I knew how Eva felt about it, I decided it wasn't so bad. "It good. I go with others who live in Chicago and need to learn English," I replied.

"Who is your teacher?"

"Her name is Camilla. She is kind. She will let me come to class anytime we are in Chicago."

"Do you find the class easy or hard?" he continued.

"It easy. Not too much homework," I said. "I think because most people working, she not give us much work outside class."

We drove in silence. It was a beautiful day, and for several miles we both enjoyed the breeze coming through the windows and the blue, cloudless sky. After a few miles, I spoke.

"Father, can I ask something?"

"Of course, anything Sam."

"I think Marlene angry at me for watching Spanish television. I think that is why she signed me up for the class. Did I do something wrong?"

Father Ron laughed. "No. I am quite sure you did nothing wrong. I think she thought *she* was doing something wrong. Parents sometimes get frustrated when they think their own kids are watching too much television, and she was probably just reacting in her normal way. I'm sure she doesn't know you don't watch TV here. Also, I think the class is something she feels will help you, which is another pressure parents put on themselves; helping their kids learn and grow."

"But I am not her kid," I replied.

"No, but she cares for you deeply."

"I thought she was mad," I said, mostly to myself, but loud enough so he could hear. Also, I found Father Ron's explanation odd. Why did Marlene care about me? I'm not part of her family, and besides, the whole reason I'm even involved is to help Juan, not go to school. Father Ron must have noticed my confusion.

"For what it's worth, I agree with Marlene that English class is good for you," he said.

"I'll do my best to learn," I promised, and this time I meant it. I wanted Father Ron to be proud of me, but mostly, I wanted to impress Eva.

"Sam, if your English improves, you could help us translate when we host the sponsors next year."

Father Ron left the car to run another errand, and when he returned, he said he wanted to stop at the store on the trip home. He asked me to help him because he was buying ice cream, and we would need to load it quickly and get back to NPH before it melted. It was a special treat that he sometimes gave to all the children.

Back in the car, I headed through town. I was still thinking of Eva. Father Ron was quiet. He told me sometimes he prayed on our rides, and I guessed he was doing it now. Maybe he was praying the ice cream wouldn't melt.

Traffic was heavy, and I was worried about getting out of the city. Now I was praying the ice cream wouldn't melt. My hands were tight on the steering wheel as we crawled along. I leaned to the left, trying to see what was holding us up, and traffic was stopped as far as I could see. Suddenly, Father Ron gasped, and by the time I got my eyes back on the road, it was too late. I had hit the car in front of us. We both jolted forward, but the seatbelts kept us in place. I looked over to see if Father Ron was hurt, and he said, "Sam, are you okay?" I knew he meant it, that he cared for me, but I could also tell he was mad. I had never seen him angry before, and it surprised me.

We both jumped out of the car. Father Ron told me to stay back as he went over to talk with the other driver. I checked the damage to our car. It wasn't a bad crash, but the headlight was broken and the front bumper scratched.

Father Ron exchanged information with the man, who seemed mad as well. He was making gestures with his arms as he yelled and pointed to his bumper. After some time, Father Ron returned.

He was still mad. As I started the engine, he said, "Sam, I have told you time and again to pay attention when you're driving."

"Yes, Father. I am sorry."

"Do you think we can drive the car back to NPH?" His voice was different than it usually was.

"Yes. I think it will drive," I answered, knowing the accident was my fault. I was hoping that this wouldn't mean the end to my driving privileges. I also felt awful for the man whose car I hit. I didn't blame him for being mad at me. I wished Father Ron would have let me talk to the man and apologize.

We didn't say anything the rest of the way home. I ran the ice cream to the cafeteria while Father Ron summoned Olegario to look over the damage.

After a discussion with both of them, I went to my room and laid down in my bunk, wondering if I would ever drive again. I decided to stay there for the rest of the night. No ice cream for me. That was all I could think of to punish myself.

\#

♪

CHAPTER NINETEEN

MARLENE
THE SOUND OF MUSIC

Oh my God, that song. I've heard it over and over. He must play it 50 times a night. I know I've heard the beginning at least that many times because he starts over every time he makes a mistake. I hear it in my sleep. I find myself humming it in the shower. What makes some melodies stick, the ones you repeat over and over in your head without even realizing?

I looked over my shoulder and saw Juan in the family room with his new guitar. The intern at the hospital who had played with him at Easter had given it to him as a gift. He loved that thing, carrying it around the house, taking it wherever he went. Because he couldn't travel with it, he was all the more excited to play every time he returned to Chicago.

The junk he collected in the living room never got picked up without a fight, but the guitar he could carry everywhere. I'd find it leaning against the couch next to him, even while he was sleeping.

I assumed he didn't want any of us to put our hands on it, but people do that with guitars. They pick them up out of curiosity even if—or maybe especially if—they don't know how to play. Just like we lip sync to our favorite songs, we feel compelled to put a guitar on our lap and strum it, even if we don't know the first thing about making music.

Maggie, too, had noticed Juan's attachment. "Mom, he sure loves that guitar. He's playing it all the time and then writing in that green notebook," she said one day as she sat at the kitchen table coloring.

I also noticed the notebook, and it made me curious. Was he writing about his experiences here? I really wanted to know, but I didn't ask. Brian had warned me about asking too many questions. I like to know things, and so I ask a lot of questions. But Brian thought that with Juan and Sam, asking too many questions might cause them to shut down and not talk at all. He was usually right about these things, so I limited my questions to only those things I really needed to know.

I was at the sink washing dishes after dinner one night, once again imagining what Juan and Sam's lives had been like as children. The visions in my head were made up ideas about their upbringing, the living conditions when they were babies, and the problems their families endured. I tried to put myself in their shoes. In their parent's shoes. How bad was it? Were their parents ever kind to them? And what had their parents endured as children? Did Juan and Sammy like the orphanage? Was it happier than life with their families?

It led me to wonder about their interpretations of their visits to the States, and specifically, time spent with my family. How did they view me? Did they like my kids? Did we have any effect on their lives? One thing was for sure, these boys were having a profound effect on ours.

Lost in my thoughts, Maggie's arrival startled me as she plopped onto a stool at the kitchen island. "I can't decide which picture to use."

She needed a baby picture for her class project, and I had dragged the bin of photo albums down from the attic for her. She had been flipping through the pages on and off all day.

Sam sat down next to her, "Let me see," he said.

Together they started paging through each book, laughing at the funny poses, crazy expressions and the hairdos Brian and I had in our younger days. "Why you wear oven mitts on feet?" he asked, laughing.

"To pretend I was ice skating," she replied and quickly turned the page. "Here I am in the pool."

Sam started laughing as he pointed to her with the hose. "You spraying yourself."

"I was just a baby."

"Look at the food on your face," he continued.

"That was birthday cake. I was only one."

They continued looking and talking. There were photos of Maggie running down the hallway in her diaper, Brian throwing her in the air. In one, she had one leg over the crib, obviously trying to escape. They were both laughing, and I was loving the interaction. I washed the same dish over and over to have a reason to stay there, not wanting to interrupt.

"You think this is so funny," she said. "I want to see your baby pictures."

Sam stopped laughing. "There are no pictures of me as baby."

"What? Why not?" she asked. I realized what he was saying. Of course, orphans didn't have baby photo albums. But at her age, how could Maggie have known?

"No camera. No mother," was all he answered.

"No one ever took a picture of you? Never?"

Sammy's eyes dropped as he quietly shook his head.

I wanted to turn around and smooth over the conversation, but I resisted. It wasn't my place, and I also realized this conversation—honest, nonjudgmental and real—was good for both of them.

Then, Sammy's eyes came up to meet Maggie's. "No. There no way to take picture of me. My first picture happen at orphanage," he said. His tone was almost apologetic.

The answers to so many of my questions came in stories like these. I had seen the NPH home. Everything these children had—their entire material world—was housed in small lockers. On our tour, one child showed us a few photos, all of them pictures from his sponsors or his life at the orphanage. But without exception, there would be few, if any, photos of these children before they came to NPH.

Most of the children had come from extreme poverty. Some had lost their parents. Others had families too poor to feed or care for them, so they left their children at NPH knowing they would be safe, well cared for, fed and educated. I couldn't imagine how difficult it would be to make the decision to give up your child—your flesh and blood, someone you loved more than anything in the world—because you couldn't provide for their basic needs.

The things we take for granted—food, clean water, safety—were only a dream for these kids and their families. Leaving them at NPH was the greatest gift these parents could give to their children; a "gift" I could not comprehend, and one that I'm sure brought tremendous heartache. But for these kids, it was a gift that likely saved their lives, or at the very least, gave them a chance at having a life of their own.

I recalled a homily Father Ron once gave about poverty. He explained that no one sitting in the audience that day could truly understand the concept of poverty. He said that even if we gave away everything we had, lived with those most in need and suffered just like them, we would never really know true poverty because we have the option to reverse course, go home to family or friends who would take us in and restore our lives. True poverty means you do not have that option.

"Why don't you have a family?" Maggie asked.

"I was born sick," Sammy said with no emotion or attachment to his statement. He didn't seem irritated or afraid to tell her his story, and I wondered if it was because he was trying to separate himself from his past. "My mom was afraid I get the other kids sick, so she throw me in garbage."

I felt my spine tense, and I slowly continued washing the dish, staring into the sink. I wanted to jump in, but before I could, Sammy continued.

"I was picked up by garbage truck and thrown into dump."

"You were in the trash? Yuck," Maggie replied, mesmerized by his story. "How did you get out?"

"A man was there, digging for food. He say he saw little hand

and dug to find me wrapped in blue blanket. He was surprised I alive. He carried me home to his wife, and they took me to the hospital. The doctors fix my stomach problem, and then I go and live with that man and his wife."

"So, you did have a family," Maggie stated.

"Yes, I guess, for some time," Sam was thoughtful in his answers. I assumed he had a vision of what his life was like then. "Jorge was like my dad. But then he was killed."

"How did he die?" she asked. She was locked in and couldn't get enough information about Sammy.

"We delivering bread. Men robbed us. They shot Jorge. Shot me here on my head." Sam showed her a scar on the back of his head. She shuffled on the stool, climbing up to get a good look at it.

I couldn't resist any longer. I dried my hands and went to look at Sam's scar. He was willing and comfortable showing us his head.

"Jorge drove me to hospital. He die but I live. Then they send me to orphanages and then to NPH." Sam was done. He sat up straight. Without missing a beat, Maggie moved on.

"Okay. Well let's get back to choosing my picture," she said. "I have to take this in tomorrow." She was clearly less affected than I was.

I grabbed his hand. "I am so sorry this all happened to you." It was all I could say. Tears filled my eyes. Sam simply smiled and returned his attention to Maggie and the photos.

I went to the living room to sit down, feeling like I needed some distance to process what I had just heard.

Juan was lying on the couch, playing the guitar. It was time for his medicine. I had devised a chart with columns for days and rows for times of the day so I could list out the medicines he had to take. I made him cross out the lines as he took each dose. I wanted him to take part in his care.

I sat down and pretended to listen, still stunned by Sam's story. Slowly, I was drawn into the music Juan was playing

"That's a different song," I commented as he finished. "What is it?"

"It's the NPH song," he said, putting down his guitar. He scooched to the edge of the couch, getting ready to take the next round of pills.

I could tell he still wasn't feeling well after his surgery. From the last few visits, I recognized the signs and could tell the moment he wasn't in pain anymore.

"Can you play it again?" I asked. He wasn't in any mood to talk.

Juan positioned himself back in the corner of the couch with his guitar. This was his post, nestled into our sectional. I noticed excitement in him, even though he wasn't feeling well. He positioned his hands, checking the strings on his left and the placement of his right hand on the base. I noticed he used a long fingernail as a pick. (I hate long fingernails on men.)

"*Cada dia al despertar. Cuando veo el sol brillar. En mi Corazon, yo siento una dulce paz, Agradezco al Padre Wasson por esta. Oportunidad de brindarme una familia y hogar….*"

I had no idea what it meant, but the sound of the song was gentle and happy. In fact, Juan smiled as he sang it, one of few smiles I'd seen from him recently.

Sam walked into the room with Maggie in tow. Sam was smiling too.

When Juan finished, I clapped. "That was beautiful. What does it mean?"

"It about Father Wasson. A thank you for bringing us brother and sisters together."

"It's beautiful." I said. "Juan you play so nice." Sometimes I found myself talking to the boys in short spurts like they did to me. In my head, I rationalized maybe it was easier for them to understand, but in reality, I think we sometimes pick up the speech patterns of the people we are with.

"Did you write the song?" I asked.

Before he could answer, Sam interjected. "No, four girls—*pequeñas*—they write it long time ago."

I turned to include Sammy—and by extension, Maggie—into

the conversation. "Do you sing it often at home?"

"Yes," Sam replied.

I thought about all the anthems that mean so much to countries, colleges and other groups. And while I didn't understand the words, I could tell this song meant a lot to Juan, Sammy and the kids at NPH, past and present.

"Was this the song you were playing at Shriners with the young doctor?" I asked.

"I try. But no, we play other songs."

I started to get up from my chair to return to the kitchen when Juan continued. "You not there." I turned to see he had put the guitar down, and his eyes were serious.

"No. We were in Florida."

"You promise to be there," he said, his gazed fixed directly at me, looking through me.

I realized I had made that promise, but to me, it was more of a promise to always be with him in spirit, even if I couldn't be there in person. But now, I realized he took it literally. I didn't know what to say.

"I'm so sorry Juan."

He grabbed the guitar and went to his room.

In bed that evening, my guilt resurfaced. It never occurred to me he would take my promise so literally. He didn't understand that I couldn't control the timing of his surgeries. Or that I had other commitments besides him. I assumed he would be fine without me. He never seemed that attached to me—to anyone—anyway. But that night, I started to understand him. He relied on me more than I'd imagined, and for someone like Juan, someone who has been through so much and been let down so often, broken promises carried a deeper meaning. Small things were important.

I couldn't sleep thinking about it. After a couple of hours, I decided to go down to the kitchen. Sitting at the counter drinking a glass of milk, I realized I was humming the NPH song. I thought about how music connected people. Songs, even without an understanding of the words, can move us deeply. It gave me an idea, and that idea gave me a new purpose. I finished my milk and went back to bed knowing exactly what I was going to do.

In the office the following week, my phone buzzed, and I hit the intercom button. "Nick Vitogiannes is here for you," Robin, the receptionist, announced.

I had worked with Nick for years on client projects. He was a true musician who wrote, produced, played and provided some great jingles and music for our campaigns. He was also a friend.

"Great. I'll be right out." I practically jumped out of my chair, but then stopped myself. I took a deep breath and walked calmly out of my office toward the lobby.

I figured Nick thought I had a client project for him. And for today's meeting, I let him believe the same because I wanted to be face-to-face for this conversation, to have him as a "captive audience," so to speak.

We hugged and walked to my office talking pleasantries. Nick was producing a new show and telling me about his plans. Outside of his day job, he produced live shows with various music themes. It was his passion. I assumed he would someday do it as a full-time career.

"So, you didn't invite me here to have me tell you about my new show," he said as he took a seat in my office. "What's on your mind?"

"I need to tell you a story first," I said.

Nick sat back in the chair. "This ought to be good," he said, cocking one eyebrow.

I not only respected Nick's talent as a musician and producer, I loved his dedication and drive, and that gave me confidence in what I was about to do.

"Over a year ago, we hosted two boys from an orphanage in El Salvador during a trip with their music troupe. After four days, I fell in love with the organization, Nuestros Pequeños Hermanos, and called them to see what I could do to get involved." I was being intentionally vague, but when I added a smile as punctuation, Nick already knew he was part of the "what" in "what I could do."

Nick leaned back, and I continued. "Anyway, I asked if I

could help them with their marketing and fundraising, and now I am on the NPH Board."

"Of course you are," he laughed.

"Brian and I even went to the international board meeting in El Salvador," I explained.

"And?" He was curious.

"When we returned, we were asked to host a boy named Juan who was having his cleft palate repaired at Shriners Hospital. He needed a series of surgeries because his cleft was so severe, and it was never repaired when he was a child."

"He's with you now?" Nick asked.

"Yes, along with a companion from the orphanage named Sam," I replied. I could feel him processing.

"Two El Salvadoran boys?"

I continued. "Juan has had three surgeries so far. During the last one, he was in the hospital and a doctor, a young intern, discovered Juan could play guitar. I guess he learned in the music program at the orphanage. Anyway, this doctor gave him one of his guitars, and now he plays nonstop."

"So you want me to work with him?" he asked.

"No, not exactly," I took a deep breath. "See, he plays a song that is the theme for the orphanage. They have homes in nine countries, supported by fundraising in the U.S. and Europe. I was thinking that maybe if someone could record that song, especially if it was sung by one of the orphaned children, it could help their efforts. They could use it as part of their marketing; sort of an anthem to support their videos and other programs."

"So *that's* where I come in." Again, Nick smiled, but this time, he leaned forward. I knew I had piqued his interest.

"Exactly. I was hoping you could donate the studio and record Juan singing it." I took another deep breath and sat back.

"So he can play and sing?" Nick asked. "Even with a cleft?"

"I can't tell you if he's any good," I shrugged, "but I think he sounds good in my living room."

"We'd want some studio musicians to bump up the quality

and production value." Nick was already producing this thing; a good sign.

"Of course, you know best. You're the expert," I replied, trying to keep my excitement in check. "Maybe you could meet with him? If it's too much, I completely understand."

That was a lie. I knew once Nick was in the studio and started working on it, he'd be hooked.

"Let me take him to the studio. I want to see how he sounds, how he plays. I am not promising anything."

Juan had no idea about this plan. I was afraid to tell him. I realized from his response about me not being at the hospital that I could not promise something unless I knew I could deliver.

That evening, Juan was lying on the couch as I explained the idea. He sat up and drew the guitar close to him, holding it by the neck. Then, he started to drum his fingers on his stump as we talked; something I noticed he did when he was excited or nervous.

"Do you want to do this?" I asked.

He nodded at first. "Yes, *sí*." He was smiling wider than I'd ever seen.

"We'll have to wait a week for your mouth to heal, and then we can schedule a time with Nick," I said.

I hoped neither Nick nor Juan would end up being disappointed.

Five days later, Juan and I were driving to Nick's studio, where the two would meet for the first time. My phone rang. It was Nick.

"Are you close?" he asked.

"Two minutes out."

"Great. When you get here, I want you to introduce us and then leave."

I was surprised, and frankly, taken aback. "You don't want me to stay?"

"No. I want the first session to be just Juan, me and the two musicians," he said firmly. "I'll drop him back at your house when we're done."

I reluctantly agreed, and moments later, we were in the parking lot outside the studio.

In a previous conversation, Nick asked me about Juan's English. Even though he was still learning the language, I assured Nick he could understand, and they shouldn't have any issues communicating. But now, as we entered the building, I was nervous. We had barely opened the door when Nick greeted us warmly and took us back to meet the other musicians. "My sister will be on drums. She speaks some Spanish if we have any issues," he said, helping waylay one of my fears. When we reached the studio, I set down Juan's guitar in a new backpack-style case Mary Jo had bought him. Juan was holding his green notebook.

"Juan, this is Nick. Nick, Juan."

Nick shook Juan's hand, said a quick hello, introduced the other musicians and promptly led me to the door. He wasn't kidding when he said he wanted me to leave.

When I got home, I was nervous, and when I'm nervous, I do housework. For the next two hours, I picked up toys, dusted and did two loads of laundry. Sam and Maggie watched *America's Funniest Home Videos* in the living room, a perfect show for them to watch together; a show where language was no barrier to its entertainment value.

For Sam, it was funny to watch someone falling down the stairs or a cat jumping at a light reflecting off his owner's watch. Maggie loved that stuff, too. So, every night after dinner, the routine was the same: hop on the couch, watch and laugh. What made me happy was the unexpected bond between those two, and with all the attention given to Juan every day, it was nice to see Sam getting positive attention and being allowed to just hang out.

As the evening progressed, everyone drifted off to their respective bedrooms until it was just Murphy and me. The kids had an early bedtime, and shortly after they went up, Sammy decided to go to his room as well. Around nine, Brian turned in, saying he had an early shift the next day.

So, there I sat, but not for long because every time I saw

headlights, I'd pop up to look out the window. I tried watching TV but didn't find anything I liked. I tried reading, but I couldn't focus. Finally, around 10:30, a car pulled into the driveway, and before they could even get out of the car, I had swung open the front door.

"How did it go?" I asked, standing on the porch steps.

Juan nodded and smiled. "Good."

He turned to thank Nick, something he rarely did. I knew things had gone well. Juan hobbled past me and into the house, immediately going upstairs to his room.

"Well?" I asked Nick after Juan had left us.

"Do you know what's in that green notebook?" he asked.

I had no clue. "No, why?"

"Well, he's more talented than I expected," Nick said. "The two musicians with me at practice played the NPH song a bunch of times. It's basic. Nice, I guess. We recorded it, and it sounds pretty good."

"That's fantastic." I was relieved that it had worked. "But did it really take you that long just to record the NPH song?"

"No. When we were done recording, Juan pulled out the notebook. He writes his own music, Mar. And the notebook is filled with songs, *his* songs."

"Really?" I had no idea.

"And they're good," Nick continued. "We jammed for two hours, learning and working on some of them."

"Maybe that's the stuff he plays here while he's sitting on the couch," I said. "There's one melody that sticks in my head. He plays it over and over."

Nick turned for the door, but before he left, he said, "I want to work with him again if you don't mind. I think everyone there and maybe some others would come back to jam and work on his songs."

"Sure, I guess," I gave a shrug. I had to let what Nick was telling me sink in. Juan's story was compelling even without the music. He had a way of drawing people to him. It was often like quicksand, you could almost hear the sucking sound of people around him getting pulled into his world.

But this was different. This time, someone from the outside, someone objective, a professional in his field, saw something in Juan and wanted to help him pursue it.

It was another night of little sleep for me. But this time, my nerves turned into excitement as I processed it all, my mind racing with ideas.

#

&

CHAPTER TWENTY

SAMUEL
FUNNIEST HOME

"**Y**ou have the funniest laugh," Maggie said through her giggles as she pointed at me. We were watching our favorite show, where people film themselves doing stupid things. Juan was gone, and I was so happy to just stay here and watch television.

"It funny," I pointed to the television. I loved this show, and watching it with Maggie was even more fun. I didn't need to understand all the English to enjoy it.

Maggie was a cute little girl. She made me feel more at home than anyone else in the family. She was almost always happy, like the kids at NPH, and just like the little ones at NPH, I'd help Maggie—and sometimes Matt too—with things around the house. It reminded me of helping the children of NPH, where we cut their food at dinner or carried their trays to the table. For me, that was fun and made me feel like I was helping, even though sometimes I could tell Marlene wanted them to do things for themselves.

At NPH, I liked to spend time in the baby house because that was Eva's work assignment. The older girls cared for the little ones, playing games, teaching them how to brush their teeth or walking them to Saturday night mass. When I was free, I helped out.

"How do you say 'laugh' in Spanish?" Maggie asked.

"*Risa*," I said. "Don't you study Spanish in school?"

"Yes." She answered. She pretended to be mad that I didn't know, but I could tell she was joking.

At the commercial, I quizzed her. "You should know lots of words in Spanish by now. What am I sitting on?"

"I don't know that one," she said.

"*Silla*. It means chair."

"OK, I'll learn more words in Spanish, but you don't know everything in English," she replied. "What's this?" She pointed to the lamp.

"Lamp," I said, glad she picked something I knew.

"Okay," she jumped off the couch. "And this?"

"Stairs," I said, replying, "What is that in Spanish?" She ignored me, deciding instead to keep quizzing me.

"What about this?"

"Desk," I said.

"How about this?"

I didn't know.

"Ha! It's a doorknob," she said, laughing and happy that she stumped me.

Then, it was my turn. "Okay, do you know what that is in Spanish?"

She looked at the door. "Nope."

She marched out of the living room. I hoped I hadn't made her mad for real. But a minute later, she came back, carrying a square pad of yellow paper and a marker.

She sat down next to me. "Let's put words on paper. I'll write the English word, and you write the Spanish one. Then we can both learn."

"How?" I asked.

"We stick them onto things," she said. "These are Post Its. They stick to stuff."

"Post it?" I asked. I had never seen papers with glue on the back.

She pointed toward the front porch. "Start at the door."

I wrote down "*la puerta*" on the paper, and she wrote "door," and then ran over to stick it on.

Soon, we had tagged things all over the house: the refrigerator (*refrigerador*), the milk (*leche*), the computer (*computadora*), a book (*libro*). Everything had little yellow stickers.

Marlene walked in and stopped to look at the note on the door. "What is this all about?"

"Learning Spanish and English," Maggie said.

Marlene laughed and told us it was a great idea. Then, she sat down and watched. I could tell she loved watching us spend time together. "Sammy, *café*?" she asked. I nodded as I wrote it on one of the yellow squares and stuck it to the coffee maker.

When I returned to NPH, I told Eva about the time I spent teaching Spanish and learning English with Maggie because she loved hearing stories about her.

One day, Eva asked me, "Do you like them?"

I had never really thought about the family in that way. They were just temporary, and I would never see them again once Juan was finished with his surgeries. I was just a guest.

"I guess I do like them," was all I replied. But in my mind, and in my heart, I think I loved them...like a family.

♭

CHAPTER TWENTY-ONE

MARLENE
NEW RULES

"**W**hat do you mean, Juan can't find his passport?" I said, turning around from the sink and looking at Sam.

"He no can find," Sam repeated sheepishly.

"Well, he must have had it at the airport. He showed it to Customs, right?" I was getting more frustrated by the second. "Brian!"

Sam just stood there like a statue. Even though it wasn't his fault that Juan couldn't find his passport, I knew he felt responsible. Again, I called for my husband. "Brian! Can you come here?"

Brian entered the kitchen from the garage, and after being told about the situation, he repeated the same exchange I'd just had with Sam. "Do you remember him showing the passport to the Customs agent?"

Then I chimed in, getting impatient. "Sam, you usually carry both passports in your backpack. Did you check it?"

The boys had arrived an hour earlier and already we were in upheaval.

"I already look," he replied. He still hadn't moved from the time he walked into the kitchen to give me the news.

"Did you take it from Juan after Customs?" Brian asked. "Where is he, anyway?"

"He upstairs." I could tell Sam felt guilty, and I sensed panic. He stared ahead and answered each question quietly.

"Juan! Get down here," Brian yelled.

Juan came down the stairs without his legs and hopped up on the kitchen stool. He said nothing. Sam was still standing in the entryway.

Brian directed the same questions to Juan.

"I don't know," was all he answered. "Sam supposed to take passports."

"But do you remember giving it to him?" Brian asked.

Juan simply shrugged.

Brian sighed, gathering himself. "Let's go and take a look through everything," he said as he turned and walked to their room. Both boys followed.

I paced in the kitchen as I listened to Brian telling the boys to check different spots. "What about the pockets of the luggage?"

"What were you both wearing on the plane?"

"Sam, where is your backpack? Juan where is yours?"

In my heart, I knew that Sam had probably checked and rechecked every possible spot before he came to tell us. He took his responsibilities and duties very seriously.

Before Brian hit the bottom of the stairs, I was already thinking about the next step.

"Should we go to the airport?" I asked.

"Let me make a call to the police desk," he said, already dialing his cell. "Maybe I'll know someone on duty." After 25 years in the Chicago Police Department, it seemed like Brian knew anyone and everyone connected with law enforcement.

He was on the phone when Sam came back down, and together we listened as Brian explained the situation to a sergeant on duty at O'Hare. Luckily, they knew each other.

Sam couldn't look me in the face, but when I glanced over at him, he looked sad and defeated. I walked over to him and whispered, "Don't worry, we'll figure it out."

"What will happen to us if I lose his passport?" he asked.

"Father Ron told me we could not lose. Now Brian call police."

"I don't know," I answered, still listening to Brian. Suddenly, I realized why Sam was scared. He had heard the word "police" and I knew he thought something really bad was about to happen.

I spoke softly to Sam, still trying to keep one ear on Brian's side of the conversation. "Sam, they won't arrest you or anything like that. We will just have to file some paperwork or work with the Consulate to get a new one," I smiled. "I'm not exactly sure how, but we will fix it. Don't worry."

Sam's shoulders visibly relaxed. This seemed to ease a bit of the guilt he was feeling. He looked down and suddenly blurted out, "The man who helped us with our bags was Anthony."

Brian heard him, relayed this new information to the sergeant and hung up. "The officer on duty will check lost and found, the Customs Office, talk to the skycap and call me back," he said.

"Sam, you guys have to be more careful with these documents. They're important, and losing them can cause a lot of trouble."

Sam looked over at me and his shoulders tightened again.

"But, it's not that Sam is in any *real* trouble, right Brian?" I looked at him with that expression that husbands and wives use to send a message to their spouse to agree with what they just said. He didn't pick up on my signal and just nodded back.

"Where is Juan?" Brian asked. He walked to the stairs and yelled up for him.

As Juan reappeared, Brian started explaining again that they had to be careful. Juan never said a word. He simply looked down and seemed unaffected. Sam, however, continued to listen intently, as though his life depended upon it.

For 30 minutes, we waited. I was in the kitchen, cleaning. Sam was sitting at the counter quietly. Juan had gone back to the bedroom, saying he didn't feel well.

"How was the flight?" I asked Sam.

"Good," he replied. "No bumps."

"Well, that's good."

There was a gap of uncomfortable silence.

Sam started speaking, quickly. He had an idea. "I think maybe on his lap. He take passport in the wheelchair. We go to Customs. Anthony pushing Juan. I get passports from backpack. We show, and then I grab crutches. We come in elevator. I never put back in backpack. My passport in my pocket."

He continued retracing his steps as the phone rang. Brian answered.

"That's great. I'll be there in 30 minutes. At the station desk? Perfect. I can't thank you enough." He hung up.

"The skycap found it when he was stowing the wheelchair. He tried to find us, but we were already gone. He turned it in, but the sergeant was able to intervene before it was logged. He said we can come and pick it up," I was relieved. It looked like Sam was going to pass out.

"I come too," Sam said, and again, Brian nodded and smiled, easing the tension. They headed for the door.

The next evening, as we prepared dinner, I commented to Brian, "Just one more story in this crazy adventure."

"I think we've have had enough stories," he laughed.

I noticed that Juan had not commented or thanked Brian when he handed him the passport. He wasn't talking much to any of us. He had spent most of the day in his room. His indifference made my angry.

"Dinner's ready!" I called.

Juan was on the couch. He looked up as I was setting bowls on the table. "I no hungry."

Sam was upstairs and came down. "Can I eat in my room?" he asked. He had been quiet all day. I assumed he still felt guilty.

Matt bopped into the room. "If they aren't eating at the table, can I eat in front of the TV?"

I was deciding if I should let them, and then I stopped. I turned and yelled for Maggie without answering any of them. "Maggie! Get down here!"

As she appeared, I looked at them all. "OK, listen. We are going to eat as a family at six o'clock every night. Not in your room.

Not in front of the TV. And even if you're not hungry, you will join us at the table. Every night. Do you all understand?" I was talking loudly. I let out a sigh and turned to the kitchen. I didn't let them answer. No one said a word.

"And wash your hands," I yelled over my shoulder. Brian was in the kitchen with a big smile on his face. He nodded once and carried the bread to the table.

Juan sat through dinner, pushing a few morsels around on his plate. He said nothing and left as soon as we finished. I assumed he was angry.

On his way out, I reminded him that Nick was taking him to the studio for practice the following evening. I was surprised that even that news didn't prompt a reaction.

Things seemed back to normal the next day. Brian was reading the paper. Juan was at the studio with Nick. Sam and the kids were watching another rerun of *America's Funniest Home Videos*.

Around 8:00 p.m., the doorbell rang. As Brian opened it, Juan rushed in, moving quickly on his crutches. Nick stood outside on the porch.

"You're home early," I said, walking into the living room. Juan said nothing and walked right past to his room. I looked at him and then to Nick, who had entered the house and was standing in the foyer with Juan's guitar. Maggie and Sam were glued to the conversation. Even they knew something was up.

"What's going on?" Brian asked as he watched Juan leave the room.

"Yeah, what happened?" I added. We could see that Nick was upset. He set down Juan's guitar case in the front hall.

"Juan was terrible tonight," he started.

"Terrible? He's been practicing constantly," I said.

"No, it's not his playing. He plays fine. It was his attitude. Anything anyone asked, any suggestion they made, he lashed out at them or made a nasty remark."

"Nick, I'm sorry," I looked back toward where Juan had exited the room.

He continued. "I'm not sure I can work with him. He's combative and stubborn. He won't do anything we ask."

"What?" I was surprised. We all assumed Juan loved these sessions.

"We couldn't get him to try anything, and the more we pressed, the worse he got," Nick explained. "Finally, he flat-out refused to practice, so I said to hell with it and brought him home."

Brian and I didn't know what to say.

"I'm sorry, Mar, but I think we need a break," Nick continued. "I don't want to give up totally on him. I mean, we have a lot of great stuff. But I can't continue with him if he's going to be like he was tonight. We don't get anywhere, and the musicians are giving their time for free. It's not fair to them, and we're all frustrated."

I looked to Brian. "Nick, you have to do what's best for you," Brian said. "Don't worry about him, or us for that matter. This was always a gift and a long shot at best, and we're both so very grateful."

Nick handed us Juan's cloth backpack and turned to leave. Brian and I were apologizing as we closed the door. We had no explanation for Juan's actions.

"We need to talk with him," I said after Nick left. Brian disagreed.

"Nope. Let him sit with this. Right now, he'll want to tell his side of the story, and I don't think we really want to hear it."

I knew Brian was right, but that night, I tossed and turned in bed, stewing over it and all the work Nick had done. It was a huge opportunity; one I couldn't let Juan throw away.

The next morning, the kids were getting ready for school and Sam was eating at the counter when Juan came downstairs. No one said anything. Maybe it was for the best; too much stress for all of us. The surgeries and his recovery were enough to deal with.

I decided to focus on breakfast. I wanted to make sure he was getting good meals. After the surgery, he wouldn't be eating any solid food for a few weeks.

For the next few days, Juan was in a terrible mood. His only comment about the incident was, "They change my songs."

Juan's journey took him from NPH El Salvador to performing on a stage in Chicago.

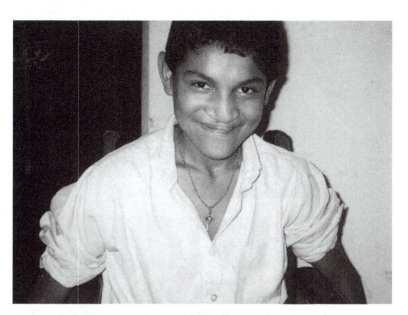

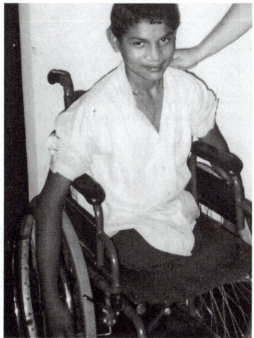

Juan came to NPH without ever having prosthetics.

Boris and Javier befriend Matt and Maggie during their fiesta tour in 2005.

The NPH music troupe performs at St. Mary of the Woods, Chicago.

Father Ron introduces the group (above), which featured Juan on percussion.

Juan arrived in Chicago in June 2006 and received his first guitar as a gift from an intern at Shriners in 2007.

Sam and Juan get comfortable with Murphy.

During his trips to the U.S., Juan receives support from Mel and Mary Jo Howard and the Byrne family.

The boys at the Byrne house Christmas 2007.

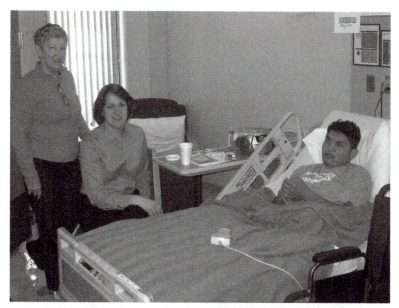

Juan recovering at Shriners Hospital, Chicago.

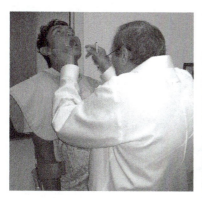

Dr. Reisberg prepping for Juan's procedures.

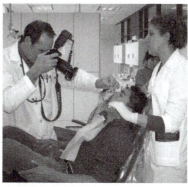

Juan's journey included getting new teeth.

Juan meets Nick and begins working on his music in the studio.

Christina in the studio.

Juan's CD, *The Sound of Gratitude,* is finished.

Guitar: Putting thanks into musical lyrics

Continued from Page 1

fire when he was 2. He turned to music — he has written 10 ballads and folk songs — and uses it to say thanks to the orphanage as well as the many people who help cover the expenses of needed facial surgeries.

"Music is one way for me to say thank you," Manuel said through an interpreter after receiving the guitar. "I'd like to teach other people to express their gratitude with song."

Since 2007, he has received medical help from Shriners Hospital in Chicago and from doctors at the University of Illinois at Chicago.

During visits to Chicago for treatment, he has entertained audiences at churches and marketing and talent relations assistant, said the company often helps out in situations like this to keep music going.

However, she said, the company likes to remain low-key about it.

"We are very honored to do something like this," she "We are a very philanth company and we love o things like this."

GILBERT R. BOUCHER II/gboucher@dailyheral

Juan Manuel of El Salvador will use the acoustic guitar he received Tuesday from Washburn Guitars in Mundelein to record a theme song for a network of orphanages in Latin America.

Juan's story gets media attention.

Behind the music, a will to live

After's life of struggles, a performance in Chicago opened up a new world — one of hope and family — to Juan Manuel Pineda

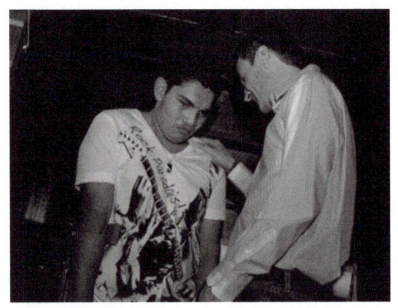

Juan's concert night began with a quiet, prayer filled moment with Father Ron.

Preparing for his stage debut with Marlene, Sam and Father Ron.

Juan takes the stage.

Juan shines on stage with performers

Nick not only produced the show but performed and brought in a talented line up to perform with Juan.

Nick Vitogiannes

Amber Tripp

Rich Perez

Chris Medina

Erica Izzo

Gina Glocksen

Steve Augeri, former lead singer of Journey, served as the headliner.

The last song.

$\textsf{\textflat}$

CHAPTER TWENTY-TWO

FATHER RON
LOSING HIS LEGS

I awoke to a clear autumn day. My window was open, the crisp air streaming over my head. I love autumn in Chicago. It was something I missed during my time in El Salvador.

For this trip back, I was serving as the visiting priest at St. Jerome Parish, saying Sunday morning masses while Father Jeremy—the regular pastor—was on vacation. Today was special, however, because I had invited Juan to sing for the congregation, many of whom were Spanish speaking.

I hoped things had improved from my visit to the Byrnes' the week before. Juan seemed crabby, but I guess that's not unusual for someone facing another surgery. Marlene had told me about Juan's opportunity to record the NPH song at the studio and to work on some of his own music with Nick and the other musicians. I knew he should be grateful but that wasn't always his immediate response to the things he was given.

On a happier note, I had received a call from the orthopedic department at Shriners. They wanted to donate a new pair of legs for Juan. His old prosthetic legs were pathetic—only the second pair he had ever received—and he had outgrown them. Not to mention, they were old technology that didn't allow for much flexion. This caused Juan to twist at the hip, swinging his legs to walk. The new version would give him bendable knees and much better mobility. I reflected on how much had happened for him after one short visit with the NPH music troupe. It reminded me that I had been asking God for so much.

Dear Lord,
Today, I recognize that my only prayers have been
to ask for what Juan needs. And you have answered my prayers
at every turn. I ask your forgiveness, and
thank you for all you have provided.
Bless those who answer your call to care for him,
treat him, teach him love.
May he learn to share his gifts with them,
and give back for all he has.
Amen.

I didn't have much time for morning prayers. I had to say three masses and wanted to review my homily. Today, I was preaching about Jesus' focus on the mild, the poor, those not first seen by him and his disciples as they walked among the crowds. The theme was a perfect match to Juan's visit and his music. The NPH children were many times the "unseen." To so many, they were invisible. Most would be on the streets, begging or worse, if not for our homes.

I was dressing for Mass in the sacristy when Brian, Marlene, Juan, Matt, Sam and Maggie arrived. Each time I saw Juan, he looked different. His face continued to show transformation and improvement. Sometimes, I couldn't remember what his face looked like before the first surgery.

"¡*Hola Padre*!" Sammy always greeted me with a hug and huge smile. Juan was quiet.

I was excited to share the news from Shriners about the new prosthetic legs, but I wanted to wait until we went to brunch after the last Mass. For now, I focused on Sam.

"Are you still attending English school?" I asked. "How is it going?"

"Very good," he replied slowly. "*Me gusta…*"

I held up my hand. "In English!"

Sam smiled. "Okay." He started again. "People in class, immigrants so much."

"Ah, they need to learn English, too," I said.

"*Sí*. I like teacher Camilla. She born in Mexico but now Chicago long time," he replied.

"I've heard a lot about her, and she sounds great," I replied, turning to the group.

Brian and Marlene were smiling. Things seemed better than during my last visit. Matt was snooping around the sacristy. Juan had taken a chair in the corner. He was looking down at his guitar case. I wondered if he was nervous.

"Juan, I have a chair and microphone ready on the side for you."

St. Jerome Parish has a bilingual congregation. The 9:00 a.m. Mass was in English, but the later service was in Spanish. I was in the back of church, lining up with the servers, and I nodded to Juan, who began playing the entrance song. As I walked up the aisle, I saw that Sam was on the end of the pew, and I touched his shoulder as I passed. He was beaming, and I realized how much I would miss our time together driving around El Salvador.

My homily flowed easily. I was always comfortable telling stories of the NPH children and explaining the homes to people. It seemed so natural to connect their lives and struggles to the Gospels.

After the homily, I sat to reflect with the congregation and looked at both Juan and Sam. My heart, my deep passion, would always be for NPH even if the church called me home. I wondered, would I remember all the stories and faces of the children I had met during my time at NPH? Would their impact fade with time? Would they remember me as they went through their lives?

I realized I was taking a bit too long in quiet reflection and stood up quickly.

Following Mass, I greeted the parishioners as they walked out. After the last had left, I went back into the church. Brian, Marlene and their family were standing with Sam.

"Father Ron, that was a lovely message," Marlene commented.

"It's easy to talk about NPH," I replied. "I love to introduce people to the homes, and it's especially impactful with Sam and Juan in the audience." As I said it, I grabbed Sam's shoulder, and he leaned into me. The NPH kids gave their affection easily once they settled into life at the home. For some kids, we could tell by their actions the exact day they finally accepted their new home and began to feel safe. It was evident when they began to give back the love to those around them.

"The next Mass will be especially impactful because it's in Spanish," I said.

"Where is Juan?" Marlene asked.

We noticed that he was still sitting up front on the chair, and when he saw us, he waved us down. As we approached, I could see that Juan's prosthetic leg was in an odd position. It seemed to be poking out from his pants leg.

"Broken," was all he said as he looked down at it.

"Let's try to get you up," Brian said, grabbing Juan under the arms.

Sam, Brian and I tried to stand Juan up, but his leg dangled below him. We would need to hold him in order to keep him from toppling to the ground.

"Let's lower him slowly," Brian instructed.

Juan began to fumble with the leg through the pocket of his pants. He was pushing it around. "It broken strap."

"Can you fix it in the bathroom?" Brian asked.

Juan looked up, angry. "No. NO! Go home."

I intervened and tried talking to him in Spanish. "Juan, can you fix it before the next Mass? Or maybe just sit on the chair and stay on the altar so you can stay and play?"

"No *Padre*. I no play," Juan insisted. "I go home."

Juan looked to Marlene, who looked from Juan to Brian to me and shrugged her shoulders. "Do we take him home?"

"*Sí. Sí,*" Juan insisted again. "I no play like this."

"I can pull the car around front," Marlene said.

Brain looked to Sam. "We will have to carry him out."

Sam and Brian got on the sides of Juan and began to lift. Matt grabbed the guitar. Juan's leg was hanging like a broken tree branch. His shoe and ankle were sticking out from the bottom of his pants leg.

"I'm really sorry about this," Brian said as they started to move.

As much as I wanted to protest, I realized there was no way Juan was going to sit in front of my next Mass, full of people, with his leg disconnected. I watched as they carried him away with Matt following closely behind with the guitar case. I knew I would have to adjust my homily.

"Sam, can you stay?" I asked as they walked to the door. "I can drop you back at the house."

"That's fine," Brian replied for him. "We can get Juan in the house."

I realized it seemed selfish, but I so wanted to make an impact about NPH in my next homily.

"Okay," Sam replied. He was always so willing to do what I asked of him.

For my next sermon, I added a short message about acceptance of things when they don't go our way. Maybe I did it more for me than the parishioners. I talked about how the congregation must not only accept those less fortunate but also act on their behalf. I realized for me, it meant accepting things that didn't always fit into my plan.

On the way to the Byrnes', Sam and I were talking and enjoying our time together. I reminded him about the time when he rear-ended another car. There were very few times we got mad at each other. Now, we were laughing about it.

When we arrived, Marlene had prepared lunch for everyone. One thing I love about their house was that it's always full of joy. Murphy greeted us at the door. Sam had obviously grown to love him and buried his face into the dog, scratching his back as he was welcomed home. Matt and Maggie were chattering and racing to the table for lunch. Marlene had obviously told them lunch wouldn't be served until we arrived. Juan had removed his legs and was sitting on the couch.

"I no hungry," he stated.

Marlene turned to me. "Juan isn't himself this week."

I went to the couch and sat next to him. On the table there were bottles of pills and a calendar listing his upcoming appointments.

"What's wrong, Juan? Are you hurt from this morning and with what happened to your leg?"

"No *Padre*," he replied. "I not feel good."

"Pain?" I asked.

"No. Stomach. Headache," he stated.

"Well, maybe my news will cheer you up," I said. "Brian and Marlene, I have something to tell you, all of you."

Marlene walked in from the kitchen, wiping her hands on a towel.

"Shriners contacted me this week," I said looking straight at Juan. "Their orthopedic department wants to fit you with new prosthetic legs." I sat back on the couch with a big smile and waited for them to react to the news. Nothing happened. I repeated my statement again, this time in Spanish.

I looked at Juan, and then to Brian and Marlene who were looking at each other. I noticed Marlene wiping her already dry hands again with the towel. The silence lingered.

Brian made the first move. "Well, that's good news, right?" He looked at Juan.

Juan was staring straight ahead. I leaned forward, with my elbows on my knees. "This is a great opportunity, Juan; a gift. Your legs are old, and these new ones will be much better."

Juan looked up at me. "With these new legs, you'll be able to bend your knees, and you will be taller, closer to the height that matches your body."

"Taller?" This additional fact did seem to affect Juan, but only slightly. After a long, uncomfortable silence, Marlene chimed in.

"Well, that is fantastic," she said. Brian was smiling at her, and I could tell they were both trying to convince themselves that this was good news.

"When will this happen?" Brian asked.

"He can get a fitting on his next visit and then, perhaps, on the visit after that he will start the physical therapy sessions to learn how to use them."

As I said it, I realized the commitment this additional treatment would put on the Byrnes, and that's when I understood their muted reaction. Juan would need rehabilitation, which meant more appointments and other care to get him walking on these new legs.

"Can we eat now?" Matt interrupted. He was obviously hungry, and I was happy to end the awkward discussion.

In bed that evening, I started piecing together the clues from the day. The leg. The pill bottles. The calendar. All the lives in that house. For the first time, I realized the extent of the commitment from everyone involved. One thing about being a priest, we saw the struggles of family and children, but we never felt the real impact because our lives were so different. More solitary. I hadn't foreseen the impact adding new legs would put on the situation. I had just been excited. I should have anticipated the family might be upset about another chore to their already busy routine with Juan.

I had one idea before I fell asleep. I would call Mary Jo in the morning. It was time to send in the cheerleader.

#

CHAPTER TWENTY-THREE

MARLENE
FEELING THE HEAT

Sometimes, I think we manufacture laundry. Every day there are piles of it. I made a mental note to remind the kids not to throw things in the "dirty clothes" basket they have barely been worn. As I sorted the piles, I noticed none of Juan's clothes were in the piles.

"Juan, can you bring down your dirty clothes?" I yelled up the stairs. "I'm doing laundry."

"I no feel good," he replied.

"Well, throw your clothes down anyway." I was frustrated with his aloofness to everyone. "If he can go up and down the stairs 20 times a day getting music off the computer, he can throw his clothes down," I thought to myself before calling to him one last time. "We'll leave for the hospital at 10."

Juan would get his second bone graft on this trip. It meant that his treatment was more than halfway complete. Once the roof of his mouth healed, the next visits would be dental and cosmetic. I felt some relief knowing we were getting closer to the end. I was weary from the experiences of the last few days. Juan's attitude wasn't good. Even my kids seemed tired of all the chaos and drama.

My mind went to a conversation in the school parking lot. I had been with a group of moms at drop-off, and we were talking as the kids lined up. Connie was listening to me talk about the boys when Kari approached. She listened for a minute and then butted in. "You're brave. I don't think I could subject my children to two strange men from another country. Are they okay?"

Before I had a chance to answer, she moved over to another group. Connie and I just stared at each other. "Unbelievable," I said, and Connie just nodded, "Don't worry about her."

At the time, I had shrugged off her comments. That night, I told Brian about the exchange, and his comment mirrored Connie's reaction. "Really? You're worried about that?" He rolled his eyes.

But even though I knew I shouldn't care, the comment had stuck in my head. I asked both kids about the boys as they got ready for bed that evening. Neither of them said anything negative about having Juan and Sammy in our house. In fact, they both acted like it was normal. "They're fine Mom," was Matt's answer.

Was it time for this to be over? Were my initial expectations too high? It certainly wasn't like I had imagined. Maybe I was just overwhelmed.

I knew the next few weeks would be hard. Juan would have the final surgery on his cleft. He would stay for an extended recovery to prevent infection. It meant more pill charts and pain management. A liquid diet. More work.

"We're here!" Mary Jo entered our house the next morning like a ray of sunshine. She and Mel were coming to the hospital with us. "This is exciting, his final cleft surgery," she said. I swear, Mary Jo could make anything sound exciting.

As she was talking, the boys came downstairs. She immediately turned to them with hugs and the same pep talk.

In the car, Mary Jo was telling us about their next travel adventure. They were off to Asia on a cruise. Each stop sounded more exotic than the last. Her mood was infectious, and I was feeling better by the time we walked in the door at Shriners.

Today, our visit was later than usual, and by the time we registered, the lobby was bursting. Children and strollers and wheelchairs were everywhere, but not in a bad way. Shriners was always such a happy and vibrant place.

As we entered Juan's room, our actions were choreographed. Juan hopped into bed, laid down and pulled up the blanket. I put his things on a shelf. Mel and Sam took his legs and crutches and put them in the closet. Mary Jo was talking about the fall weather as she opened the drapes and looked out the window.

The first nurse appeared and started checking on Juan. "Did you realize he has a fever?" she asked, looking at me.

"No." I got up and went to the bed.

"I'll be right back," she said.

After she left, I asked Juan if I could feel his forehead. I gently placed my hand on his face and realized he was warm.

I looked straight into his eyes. "I no feel good," he said quietly.

It came rushing at me. He didn't feel good at dinner. He didn't feel good with Nick. He didn't feel good this morning.

Before I could comment, Doctor Reisberg came in. "What is this I hear about a fever?" He was already feeling Juan's head, having him lie back to examine his mouth.

We all stood back.

"I'm going to get a culture and some blood work," Doctor Reisberg said. "Why don't you all stay in the waiting room until I know something?"

"I think I may have missed the signs," I said to Mary Jo as we sat in the waiting room.

"You're not a doctor," she defended me. "You're doing a great job."

Doctor Reisberg entered. "Let's all sit down," he started. "It seems our last graft has been compromised. An infection has spread into the tissue, and that is why Juan is not feeling well. We won't be able to proceed today. In fact, we'll need to remove the graft from last time and let him heal."

He could see our concern. "We will remove the bad tissue and once it heals, we'll try again. It's a bit of a setback, but this is not uncommon. We see this sometimes with cleft patients. As I told you, Juan's age makes this a more complicated process. His cleft was deep, but we'll repair it. On a more positive note, we can do some minor work on his lip today."

"Well, that's good at least," Mary Jo nodded.

"I'll work with my staff to schedule a surgery in six to eight weeks for his re-grafting."

"I'm sure it will work then," Mary Jo said.

"I'll know more once we get in there," he said as he stood up. "Okay, I will see you all after surgery." And with that, he was gone.

As soon as he left, Mary Jo took over. "I'm sure it will be fine. It's just a small setback." She grabbed my arm.

"I'll be right back," I said. I stood quickly. The tears were rolling down my face before I turned down the hallway. I was in a full sob by the time I reached the window at the end of the corridor. I didn't know if I was crying for Juan and all he had to endure or for myself and the guilt of not seeing his pain or maybe for the extension of all of this. I couldn't stop. After a minute, I felt two hands on my shoulders. It was Mary Jo. She hugged me and didn't say a word. I just let it all out.

Finally, she said, "We're here for you."

I was barely able to catch my breath. "I should have seen it. He's been complaining for days. I've been so annoyed with him. Maybe I'm not the right person to do this."

She turned toward the window with her arm still around my shoulder. Outside, a group of kids—both sick and healthy—played in the courtyard. One in a wheelchair. One with a helmet on. Another on crutches.

"Each one of those kids has had setbacks too," she said. "Their parents don't think they can do it either. But they can, and so can you."

We didn't say another word while I composed myself the best I could before returning to Juan's room. He was prepped for surgery, and everyone was chatting away.

I walked to his bedside and took his hand. It was so strong yet soft.

"I'm so sorry, Juan, that I didn't listen you," I said.

He didn't seem to care about what I was saying and asked, "You will be here?"

"Yes, I will be here the whole time," I answered.

He didn't seem happy or sad. He just nodded to confirm, closed his eyes and laid back in the bed until they came to take him to away.

#

♪

CHAPTER TWENTY-FOUR

SAM
NO MORE

"**H**ola *Padre*," I said as he entered. I had been waiting in his office for a long time.

I watched him walk around his desk. I was sitting in the chair, with my hands folded in my lap. He sat down behind the desk and put his hands together on top of a mound of papers.

"What can I do for you, Sam?" he asked.

I looked down and took a deep breath. "I don't want to go back to Chicago." I had said it. Out loud. I couldn't look at him, but it felt good to finally get it out.

For months, I had thought about this moment. I knew Father Ron and everyone else thought going with Juan was such a privilege.

But they didn't know what I knew, and what I had gone through being his caretaker. I hated almost everything. The airplane was scary. The food was different. I had to go to English school with strangers. I missed my friends and my home. And most of all, I missed Eva.

Inside, I was sick of being nice to him. Doing whatever he said. But I couldn't tell anyone about that. What would everyone think of me? Sometimes, I felt guilty just having those feelings. But they were real, and I couldn't keep pushing them down.

Father Ron just sat there, tapping his fingers on the stack of papers. I could hear the ticking of the clock on the wall, and after a few seconds, just as I was about to continue, he spoke. "I see. Why?" he asked softly. He didn't seem mad or even surprised. Then, we sat for a few more seconds. Tick, tock went the clock on the wall.

"I think, maybe, someone else should get the chance," I said. I thought that if I made it seem like I was being generous, I wouldn't have to explain my real feelings.

"So, it's just that you want to give someone else a chance, is that right, Sam?" he asked. "That's very kind of you."

I looked at the floor and nodded. I knew I couldn't look Father Ron in the eye as I told him a lie.

"Are they good to you while you stay in Chicago, the Byrnes?"

"Yes," I said. "They are nice."

"Are you learning English at Centro Romero?"

"Yes. Camilla, my teacher, is fine," I didn't want to make it about any of these things. After all, everyone in the United States had been so good to me.

"I thought you liked the classes."

"Yes. I do," I answered.

"Are you able to help Juan?"

"Yes." I didn't like where I thought this was headed, and I prepared to argue my case.

He stood up quickly. "Well, let me think about it. That will be all."

I looked up, surprised at his response. I was feeling conflicted. I had hoped he would tell me his decision. I wanted to stay, plead some more, or wait for him to say OK to my request. But none of that happened. Father Ron just ended the meeting by walking out, leaving me to sit there alone.

On one side, I felt relief. I had said what I needed to say, and he didn't say no. It meant maybe he would agree.

On the other side, I was feeling ungrateful. I was jealous of Juan. And jealousy was something I knew Father Ron hated. Most of the kids would have jumped at this opportunity. They would have been mad at me if they knew I had asked not to go back. I decided to stay quiet. I wouldn't tell anyone—not even Eva—until Father Ron made his decision.

#

♪

CHAPTER TWENTY-FIVE

FATHER RON
REBOOT

"**M**el, how are you? It's Father Ron." I realized he would be surprised to get a phone call from El Salvador.

"Father Ron? I didn't know you were in Chicago," he replied.

"I'm not," I said. I could hear Mary Jo in the background asking the same thing. "I'm calling from El Salvador because I need to talk with you about Juan." I continued by telling Mel about a conversation I'd had with Juan.

The day after the meeting with Sam, Juan arrived in similar fashion. I was working at my desk when he came in and hopped up on one of the chairs across from me, the same chair Sam occupied the day before. Fumbling with his hands and staring at the ground, Juan had asked if he, too, could stop going to Chicago. Was this a conspiracy? I sat back and took a deep breath to listen as he explained…sort of.

"I don't want my face fixed more," he said. "I think I am good. I am better than I was before. Good enough." I just sat back and listened, as if I was contemplating what he was telling me.

In reality, I was strategically slowing down the pace of the conversation. After he finished, I did what I always do when someone gives me bad or surprising news. I sit for a moment. And then, slowly and contemplatively, I speak.

"But Juan, you understand that the roof of your mouth is not repaired, that the surgery wasn't successful," I explained. "It's open again and needs to be finished. It's important for your health."

"I think it is good," he said with as much positivity as he could muster. "My lips look better, and I think this is all I need."

I let him continue, to try to convince me. I knew he would never really tell me what this was all about. Again, I sat back in my chair, letting it sink in, letting him sit there uncomfortably as he awaited my response.

"Let me think about it," I said finally, and like the day prior, I ended the meeting and walked out, leaving Juan sitting there. I knew I needed to investigate, to find out what was really going on. So, I called Mel and Mary Jo.

"Mel, tell me what's going on with Juan. How is everyone doing up there?" I asked. "I know there was a problem with his graft, but how did everyone take it?"

I hadn't planned to tell anyone in Chicago or El Salvador about my meetings with Sam and Juan. I had fought so hard to get approval from the NPH team in the first place, and I certainly didn't need to fight a battle on that front right now. Rather, I needed to gather information about everyone involved to plot my next steps. I knew there must be something I could do to keep this entire thing from blowing up. I blamed myself too, for being busy and detached from the situation.

"Well, when Juan arrived last time, I think he wasn't feeling well from the first day. Sometimes, it's hard for Marlene or any of us to really know what he's thinking."

"Yes, he can be difficult that way," I replied.

"He's not the best communicator," Mel laughed. "I don't think Marlene—or the rest of us for that matter—saw the signs. She felt pretty devastated when we found out right before they were about to operate."

"The doctor said it's not a big setback," Mary Jo chimed in, and it was then I realized she had picked up the other extension.

Before I could say hello to Mary Jo, she continued. "Mar was sobbing in the hallway; she was just a wreck about Juan's condition after they removed the graft. Of course, none of it was her fault, especially since he had been back in the care of the NPH medical staff too, but she felt somewhat responsible."

"I'm sure it's not easy," I replied.

"Luckily, Doctor Reisberg was able to begin the repair of his lip instead," she said.

Then, it was Mel's turn. "How is everything going with Juan's recovery back there?"

"Juan is recovering well," I said. "All indications are that he will be ready next February."

Mel seemed to ignore both of us. "There is so much aftercare when he's released from the hospital. Pills. Rinses. Mary Jo and I help as much as we can, but most of it falls on Marlene and Brian."

"Do you think they're frustrated?" I asked. I knew I was making progress in getting the real story because usually Mel isn't so open. But this time, he was giving me some good information.

"I don't know. If they are getting frustrated, I don't think it's because of the work or the time required..."

"...it's the emotional toll it's taking," Mary Jo interrupted. "As you well know, Father, this process is painful, and Marlene worries she's not up to snuff on the medical side of his care. This infection seemed to confirm her insecurities."

"That's ridiculous," I replied. "He was here at our clinic after the graft, and they didn't diagnose the infection, either."

"I know," Mel said, always the calming influence. "I think the break will make everyone relax and be prepared for next time."

Again, Mary Jo broke in. "It'll all be fine, and we'll be there for Brian, Marlene and their family. We will spend even more time helping during the next round. Not to worry."

"How about Sam and Juan? How do you think they are doing?" I asked.

"Sam gives the impression that he's struggling with English school, but his teacher told us that he is the fastest learner she has ever taught. He's keeping up with the class even though he only attends when he is in Chicago."

"Really?"

"Yet, he seems unnecessarily disappointed in his progress," Mary Jo said. When you're talking to Mel and Mary Jo, it's kind of like being with a husband-and-wife comedy team. They tend to play off of one another and finish one another's sentences because they're so in sync. Sometimes, it made me laugh. But now, I was thrilled, getting as much information as I could get.

"And Juan?"

"He's tough," Mel said, and it almost sounded like he was talking about his own son. "This last visit was particularly difficult, and yet he really didn't open up to us about how bad he felt. I don't think he could express how he was feeling, about his illness I mean, and we all took it as anger."

"And I think he was in a lot more pain than we knew," Mary Jo said.

Mel continued. "I think perhaps Juan's feeling a bit resentful about Nick and the studio experience. Nick was so generous to offer his time and talent, but finally he had had enough of Juan's attitude and refusal to work with the musicians, and so Nick just ended it. All this happened before the news about the surgery. I think it all hit him hard."

Mary Jo added, "He's really a good kid when he's feeling good."

And there it was, the underlying reason Juan didn't want to continue.

"Do you think everyone can keep going? Or should keep going?" I asked.

"Father Ron, I would tell you honestly if I thought for a second that we couldn't or didn't want to do this. But we all do," Mel said. "Especially Marlene. I think deep down, it would crush her if you told her Juan was going to quit."

For the first time in our discussion, no one spoke. Even Mary Jo was quiet, thinking things through like me.

Finally, Mel put a button on it. "Ron, nothing we achieve, nothing really great, is done without a little anguish." Mel was like that. He didn't speak often, but when he did, it was important and generally, right on the money.

"Yes, we will be fine!" Mary Jo added enthusiastically, as though someone had just given her a shot of adrenaline. That was Mary Jo's superpower, the ability re-energize a situation. It made me smile.

"You two have given me exactly what I needed," I said. "Now, no offense Mel, but I need Mary Jo's special skills." I could feel him smiling through the phone. "Sure thing, Father. I'll leave you two to talk on your own. Take care and God bless."

"How can I help you, Father?" It was impossible to speak to Mary Jo and not feel uplifted.

"Mary Jo, I have a request, a job for you, so to speak. It's sort of a three-month mission."

I knew if she could handle Marlene, I could handle the boys. Juan wasn't scheduled to return to Shriners until well after Christmas, so I had time. I spent the next few minutes strategizing with Mary Jo how we would—on our respective ends of this adventure—re-energize both Marlene and the boys. Ten minutes later, I hung up the phone and sat back in my chair, confident that Mary Jo and I could get this train back on track.

For the next month, I didn't address either of the boy's requests. I would see them on the grounds and wave without stopping to talk. Sam would drive me places, just like normal, and we would talk endlessly about all kinds of things. I never talked about Chicago and knew neither he nor Juan would have the nerve to bring it up. They were curious but had too much respect to push me for an answer.

Time was on my side. The boys had busy schedules, endless hours of activities, chores and events would occupy their time and thoughts until February. For most of us, bad memories diminish over time, and I was hoping this was true for them as well.

Soon, it was Christmas time. I love Christmas at NPH

because unlike back in the States, here the holiday focuses on the birth of Christ and the hope his life brings to all of us. Like a breath of fresh air, the Christ story comes with meaning. Of course, there are small presents, and food, but the theme is about celebrating the start of something spectacular.

My Christmas Day homily spoke of rebirth, new beginnings and hope. I talked about accepting not only gifts from our family, but God's gifts, the ones we don't unwrap or even understand but that can mean so much in our lives.

I sat down for reflection, and instead of bowing my head and closing my eyes, I looked into the pews to find Juan and Sam. Juan was sitting on the end of the pew, staring up at the manger near the altar. Sam was next to Eva and the little ones. His head was bowed, but I could almost feel his happiness, spending Christmas with someone who meant so much to him. I hoped my message had come across loud and clear to both of them.

After the holiday, everyone was happy. Christmas had been perfect; the kids were excited and happy. It was truly a season of celebration. The only thing ever missing for me—the Midwestern boy—was snow.

Shortly after Christmas, Sam was driving me to Santa Ana. As we entered the town, Christmas decorations still dotted the streets and neighborhoods. A nativity scene was still on display in front of one of the churches, and it inspired me to ask Sam a question.

"Sam, what do you think Jesus means at Christmas?"

"He is our Savior," he replied.

"Yes," I continued. "But he was a gift, perhaps the best gift for all of us." Sam continued to drive along quietly.

"Sometimes I wonder, when Mary found out she was pregnant, what was her first thought? Do you think she was nervous or unsure about accepting her incredible gift? I mean, how did she feel?"

Sam didn't answer. He just stared straight ahead, keeping his eyes glued to the road. (After our accident some time ago, he rarely broke his focus on the road ahead of him.)

I continued. "Life is like that. We get opportunities, but

sometimes we don't see what a gift they are right away." I could see his hands tighten on the steering wheel, and I wondered if he was wise to what I was getting at. I didn't wait to find out.

"Sam, your opportunity in Chicago—and with Juan—is a gift, too. It might not seem like it now, but I promise it will someday, maybe sooner than you think."

I let it sink in, sat in silence, and then I continued. "I want you to accept what God has offered with this opportunity. I want you to see it as a gift. I believe in my heart it will become invaluable to you in the future. It will be perhaps the best gift of all."

Sam nodded. I knew he would see it through, not necessarily because he agreed, but at least out of respect for me and what I was telling him.

"And, Sam, I have one more request. When you go back to Chicago, embrace the opportunity you have in front of you. Keep studying English. Be part of the Byrne family. Engage with them. And open your heart to Juan. I know that might be hard, but please do your best. Oh, and enjoy this time because it will be over quickly."

"Yes Father," he replied as he stopped to let some pedestrians cross the road. It was then he looked at me and smiled.

"You don't return to Chicago until February," I said. "When you do, put your heart into the opportunity, and I promise you will receive benefits."

When we arrived at our destination, I asked Sam to wait in the car while I ran my errand. It would be time alone for him to ponder my request.

Juan appeared at my door on New Year's Day. I had asked him to come see me after breakfast. I waited until he hopped up on the guest chair before I spoke.

"Juan, I have something for you," I said as I handed him a wrapped package.

He was surprised and slowly reached out to take it. He looked at me with an inquisitive face. I didn't give individual presents to any of the *pequeños*. When I bought things for the kids, it was usually ice cream or a field trip for all who wanted to go.

"Open it," I said.

As he unwrapped it, I continued. "Juan, do you remember the first time you arrived in Chicago?"

"Yes," he replied as he revealed the gift, a wall calendar.

"Do you know how many times you have been back there?"

He had to think for a minute, "Five?"

"Actually six," I said. "Does it seem like a long time or not so much?"

He shrugged, "Not too much, I guess."

"Exactly," I replied. "Things never seem to take as long when we look back at them."

He still wasn't sure what I was saying, but he nodded.

"Juan, at the start of your journey to Shriners, I told you there would be hard times. I believe the last trip was the hardest."

He listened as he paged through his gift, and I could see he was already starting to understand my purpose for the gift and this visit.

"In that calendar, I have written down the planned trips necessary to finish your treatment. They might not be exactly right, but they are close," I said. "I want you to think about how quickly the time will pass, how soon you will be done and how much better your life will be for many years because you continued this treatment and saw it through to the end."

Juan looked straight into my eyes, staring a hole right through me. He wasn't mad, but I could tell he was taking my words seriously, yet unsure if he agreed with what I had to say.

"The new year always brings new beginnings," I said. "I believe this year will bring you joy and accomplishment. I'm giving you this calendar so you can put last year behind you and focus only on what's ahead." Then, I looked him square in his dark, penetrating eyes. Now, it was my turn to look through him. "I want you to continue your treatment. I want you to have a new face, a healthy mouth and new teeth. I want you to find a positive way to move forward. And, I want you to be nice to everyone who is working hard to help you both there and here."

He was silent.

"Juan, I believe once you get over this next hump, time will go fast, and you will see the good in finishing the surgeries on your face."

I sat back in my chair, and Juan looked down at the calendar. He rubbed his hand slowly over the cover and then opened it again. He turned to February and saw the next dates for Chicago marked in pen. He closed the cover and slowly looked at me.

"OK, *Padre*," he said quietly. Then, he slowly hopped down from the chair and moved toward the door. I was about to say something, but I stopped and just let it be. He was gone.

♪

CHAPTER TWENTY SIX

MARLENE
MUSIC REPLAY

"**W**hat are you doing here," Nick asked as he gave me a hug, "checking up on me?"

Nick was working with my agency's creative team on a new jingle for a client. In the studio, Nick came to life. His energy and constant pursuit of making things better made working with him a pleasure.

I was not here about the client work, but I didn't want to be obviously pushy, so I lied. I channeled Mary Jo and her positivity into my conversation with Nick.

"I'm just here to watch your amazing creativity," I said. "You know I love being in the studio with you." At least that was true.

Nick turned back to his work as I sat and watched. Creative minds work in layers. The process is like watching a building go up in fast forward. Piece by piece, you see them build, and the journey to the end result is fascinating. Each time I thought they were finished, Nick and the team would find something to tweak, and what they would add would suddenly seem obvious and make it sound much better. Soon, the team was finished, satisfied in what they'd created, for the time being, anyway. They decided to "take 10" and then return to give it a final listen.

During the break, Nick sat down next to me, drinking a pop and making small talk. Out of the blue, I mentioned Juan.

"Juan returns next week."

"Really, how is he doing?" he asked nonchalantly.

"Well, you know last time he had a terrible infection in his mouth that we were unaware of," I said. "I felt terrible that I didn't listen when he told me he wasn't feeling well. The doctor said his pain tolerance is so high from the burns he sustained as a child that he probably didn't complain like a normal person would have."

I kept talking. "They had to remove most of the graft in his mouth from the previous surgery."

"Wow, I didn't realize," Nick said.

"Yeah, he had a 102 fever when we got to the hospital that day," I said. "It was my fault for not noticing. He was sick from the moment he landed, and I didn't see it."

Nick immediately came to my defense like I knew he would. "You can't hold yourself responsible. Where were the doctors and nurses? I mean, you're not a medical professional, Mar."

"I know, but by the way he was acting, the day at church when he refused to play and then when he wouldn't work with you in the studio, I should have put it together. It was because he was so sick." I shook my head.

Then, my eyes went to Nick. He had a puzzled look on his face.

"The doctor said that if he hadn't seen him that week, it could have been serious," I continued. "They had to remove most of the repair they had done on the upper roof of his mouth and send him back home."

"That's terrible," Nick said.

"Now he'll have to come back so they can do it again," I said. "The doctors at NPH have monitored him closely for four months and believe the infection is gone."

"When does he get here?" Nick asked.

"Next week," I said.

"Oh," Nick was thinking, I could feel it. I had him. I waited a beat or two, letting the silence dominate the moment. Then, I did it.

"Do you think you might try again with him?" I asked. "Give him a second chance?" Another long silence.

"I don't know," Nick said. "He was pretty difficult last time."

"I think he was just feeling rotten, Nick."

"Well, maybe just Christina and I could set aside some time," he replied, mentioning his sister, who is a drummer and was involved in the previous sessions with Juan. "We can jam with him for fun, I suppose, and see how things go."

"That would be fantastic," I said, not hiding my excitement. "I just want him to continue with his music."

I left the studio swinging my keys, humming all the way to the car. It was that song Juan always played at our house, a song to which I knew neither the title nor the lyrics; or if it was even a finished piece.

Mary Jo would have been so proud of me. She showed up at my door the week after New Year's to take me to lunch. What is it about some people and their nurturing spirit? From the moment we sat down at the restaurant, she reminisced about the journey we had taken with Juan. Her recollection was so positive. She reminded me what he was like when he first arrived; quiet and sullen, his face malformed. She talked about the funny events we had experienced: the hot sauce tasting competition at the restaurant on their first visit; Juan's guitar playing on Easter Sunday. She talked about Sam's English skills. How he had used Post-it notes to practice English and Spanish with Maggie, and how much he'd grown throughout this journey.

By the time our food arrived, I was feeling good again—really good—about the whole process. I had forgotten the challenges.

"We will all be in a better place when Juan returns," she said. "I also think you should talk to Nick to see if he'll come back and help Juan pursue his music."

I sat there for a moment, thinking about what she had just said and if I could bear asking Nick for anything more. Then, she asked me a question: "If you don't try again with Juan and his music, do you think you might regret it once he is gone for good?"

At home that evening, I thought long and hard about that question, and the answer that kept coming into my mind was, "Yes. Yes, I would regret it. Yes, I would feel bad if I didn't do everything I could to help Juan realize his dreams, or at very least, realize that music wasn't his dream, if that were the case."

Juan's songs, especially his favorites, replayed over and over in my head for the next two days. If no one ever heard the music except for me, it would be my fault. Mary Jo was right. I could not let the opportunity slip away without a fight. If I was Juan's catalyst, she was mine, and I wasn't going to let her down.

Four weeks later, Juan was sitting in my kitchen having coffee. I always found myself drinking more coffee than I should when the boys were in town. It was an easy way for me to connect with them, and at that moment, I needed to connect with Juan. It was time for "the talk."

"Juan, when you were here last time, did you enjoy the studio music sessions at all?" I asked. "I know the last one didn't go so well."

"Yes, I like it," he replied. Juan was a different person on this trip. It was obvious he felt better than on his last visit. He was talking more and seemed polite. "But I no like when they change my music."

"What do you mean by change the music?" I asked.

"Nick changed things. He tell Christina to play it different or try new beats."

Juan was upset about the way they worked on his songs. He didn't understand the creative process.

"Do you think they were trying to make the song better?" I asked.

He shrugged.

"Nick is a professional. He works with musicians all the time. And he also works with my team on the music we create for clients. And when he does, he's always adding things and trying new ways to make the music better. And most of the time, he does," I explained.

Juan was listening carefully. He had both hands around his coffee cup, needing it to keep him warm in this February weather but also as a comfort element during our talk.

"Nick knows what to do to make songs, I don't know how to say it, more 'rock star,'" I said with a laugh. "Maybe he can help you be a rock star."

Juan smiled, but this smile was different. This time, it was a real smile, a grateful smile. One that came from his heart.

"Do you want to work with him again?" I asked.

"I was sick," he replied, giving me his version of why things had gone so wrong.

"I know," I said. "I am so sorry that when you tried to tell me, I didn't listen."

"No," he said slowly. "Yes."

I was confused. "Yes you want to practice or no?"

"No, not your fault," he explained. "Yes, I want to work with Nick. But will he want me?"

"I think he will, but you have to do as he says. And be nice," I replied with a smile. "Nice like I know you can be; like I know you are."

Again, Juan smiled, and it was the smirk I'd seen before. But this time, I understood it. I walked over and gave him a hug. It was the first time I had given him affection when it wasn't a greeting of hello or goodbye. He leaned his body against mine from the barstool. I was afraid he might fall off since he wasn't wearing his legs. I felt him relax and realized I should do this more often. After all, when it came to love and affection, Juan had a lot of catching up to do.

The following week, I was driving out to Nick's studio to pick up Juan when I realized I was gripping the steering wheel too tightly. The tension was two-fold. First, I was thinking about this session, hoping it was going well. Also, the roads were slippery. February had hit Chicago with snow, cold and ice, and no matter how many winters you spend driving in this stuff, you never get comfortable with it.

I took a deep breath and opened the door to the studio. Music blasted out, hitting my ears—my whole body—like a gust of wind. It was like walking into a wall of sound that had been completely muffled inside the building, just waiting to escape. They were obviously still practicing. I took that as a good sign.

Behind the glass, I stood in the corner and watched Nick's sister, Christina, pound the drums. She was amazing, her blonde hair flying, her tiny figure surrounded by drums and cymbals of all sizes. Nick had an electric guitar over his shoulder, and Juan was sitting on a stool with his acoustic.

He was concentrating and leaning forward on the stool, his prosthetic legs planted on the floor. After all this time, I'd finally gotten used to seeing Juan's "legs" standing underneath his body, attached but looking like they were nailed to the floor as he sat. He was over his guitar and his head was bobbing up and down to the rhythm as he concentrated on his hands working the strings.

I recognized the song. It was the one he played at home from the couch, over and over. But in here, it sounded different. Better.

The scene could not be more beautiful or perfect. I sat down quietly and observed, hoping they wouldn't notice.

In the booth, Nick's studio engineer noticed me and smiled. "I've been grabbing some tape of their session," he said. "Nick wants to hear how it sounds."

Nick had already provided the track for the NPH song. I wasn't sure what he was capturing today, but it appeared things were going well at the moment, so I didn't question it. I just sat quietly as they worked on a few more things, and then the session was over. When they emerged, Juan and Nick were both sweating through their shirts, and everyone seemed happy.

All the way home, Juan was drumming his fingers on his thighs. I wondered what it must feel like to touch a part of your body and not feel anything. His new prosthetic legs almost looked real, so much better than the old ones. They had a joint at the knee that allowed for a natural bend and were much more realistic in design. But at the end of the day, he still took them off. He was always more comfortable without his legs than with them.

"I like Christina on drums," he said.

"She's amazing," I agreed.

"Nick good on guitar, too."

"Yes, he can play," I agreed again. "You all sounded great together. Are things better with practice?"

"Yes, I can see how my songs are better," he said with a smile.

I pulled into the driveway and walked around the car to hand Juan his crutches. He slid his arms in the cuffs and grabbed the handles before lifting himself out of the car. It took him a minute before he was upright. I grabbed his guitar bag and we started for the front door.

It was only 10 or 15 feet to the porch, but somewhere on the sidewalk, I felt Juan tipping over. Then, his crutch slid out and the next thing I knew, we were falling. It was like slow motion as we went down, not slow enough that I could stop it or catch him, but slow enough that I could replay every moment. Much like in the movie when Bambi slid on the ice and his limbs went in different directions, Juan's legs had gone out from under him. In one slow, continuous, agonizing fall, his legs, the guitar and the crutches were all over the sidewalk. I fell too with my purse spilling out among everything else. I'm sure I screamed. Juan let out a sound, too, more of a grunt.

We were down on the ice in a pile. I was on my side, still gripping the guitar case. Juan was face down, one crutch under him with the strap still on his forearm. The other crutch was somewhere in the snow.

I sat up and slid over to him. "Are you okay?"

"I not hurt," he replied. "I not hurt." It was like he was telling himself.

I carefully grabbed his shoulder and he pushed up. His body rolled, and we were staring at each other, plastered with snow.

I looked at his body and he looked at mine. When our eyes met, we burst into laughter. We couldn't stop.

"What's going on out here?" Brian opened the front door. He had heard us and hurried to help.

"Are you okay?" he asked as he tried to help lift us.

"I hope so because we can't stop laughing," I replied.

Murphy had escaped, and Matt and Sam were chasing him on the front lawn. Maggie was standing on the porch.

For the next week, I laughed every time the scene came into my head.

Friday afternoon I was back in the office after spending the morning at Shriners. Juan's surgery had gone well. At least for now, it looked like this graft would take. He was recovering in his hospital room. Sam went to English school with Mel and Mary Jo. My kids were also in school. We were back to a routine.

"Nick is here to see you," Robin announced on the intercom.

"I'll be right out," I responded. I walked to the lobby wondering if I had missed an appointment on my calendar.

"Hi," I said. "Did we have a meeting?"

"Nope," he replied. "I'm just checking in unannounced like you do to me." He laughed.

Nick walked past me toward my office, and I followed him. I was thinking things had not gone well in practice, figuring I was about to get an earful from Nick.

"Did things not go well at practice?" I asked. "You both seemed happy."

Nick entered my office, and I sat down at my desk. He waited for me to walk around and sit down.

"Juan was great," Nick opened his laptop. "Listen to this."

It was Juan and his song. I smiled, "That sounds great."

"That's because it *is* great," Nick said.

I nodded in agreement but didn't know what to say next. Nick waited, until he couldn't hold back any longer.

"We have to record him," he announced.

"Isn't that a recording?" I replied, pointing to the computer.

"This was just for fun," he said, pointing at the computer. "We need to record him for real."

"Why?" I asked.

"His songs are good. His music is good. But his story is great. It's unbelievable, in fact," he said. "It needs to be heard."

I just looked at him, confused.

Then, he hit me with something I hadn't planned on. "I want to record an album of his music."

I was still staring at him as he continued.

"Not just a few songs, either. I think he has enough material for a full album. Once we get it recorded, we'll host a concert, maybe at one of the event halls here in Chicago. I don't know which one yet."

"A concert?" I said in disbelief. "What?"

"Yes. I'll get the musicians to donate their time. It will be an awesome story, and the music he has written is good. We can make something of his songs."

"Can he even play in front of an audience?" I was trying to process all this at once.

"I hope so because I asked Steve Agueri, the former lead singer for Journey, to join us at the concert," Nick continued. "We'll get him to sing with Juan and sing his songs as well. In fact, he has a new single."

"You did what?"

"And not just him. I invited Gina Glocksen and a few past American Idol performers." He sat back, smiling.

"Very funny." I replied.

"I'm not joking, Mar. This is happening," he replied, leaning forward in the chair. "Your staff will handle ticket sales and publicity. I will take care of the venue and production."

"We can't do that," I said. "I don't know anything about putting on a concert."

"You won't put on the concert, I will. And I know you, Mar, you can sell anything."

"I don't think we can do this," I argued.

"Yes, we can. And I don't know why, but I know we have to do it, no matter what it takes." Nick was speaking like it was an obligation, not a decision. He sat back in the chair. "You started this."

I sat for a moment, still stunned. "OK, but first, who should talk to Juan?" I asked.

#

CHAPTER TWENTY-SEVEN

SAMUEL
COLD SPEAK

Entering the building felt good. In just the time it took to walk from the car, under the Romero Center sign and through the door, the wind seemed to freeze my face. The weather in Chicago in February is always so cold. I have tried to explain the cold and snow to my friends at NPH, but there were no words to help them comprehend how it bites at your skin. No way to change their minds from thinking snow was soft like cotton. I used examples like ice or the side of a cold Coke bottle to make them understand, but we don't ever feel cold like this. We rarely even serve anything with ice at NPH. It's too expensive to make.

Mel had given me one of his winter coats. Even with that coat, scarf, hat and gloves, I was shivering. I looked back to see Mel waiting for me to get into the building, and he waved before he drove away. He always waited there to make sure I was in the building before he left.

I turned and walked through the lobby and Hilda, the greeter, said hi to me. She was always friendly. In fact, everyone here was always friendly to me when I came to study.

Today, I surprised Hilda and myself as I turned to her and said, "Good morning."

Father Ron had made it very clear that I needed to keep

coming here for English classes. He also had asked that I embrace the opportunity. Maybe it was time to be nicer to these people.

I thought about Juan going back to Shriners for another surgery. I decided I would not be mad about my circumstances especially when I knew at that moment he was on the operating table and would wake up in pain.

We hadn't talked much on our trip back to the U.S. I never told him I had asked to be replaced and didn't want to come back.

As I got to my desk, I started to peel off the layers of clothing; the gloves, hat, scarf, and finally the coat. There was no good place to put all of it, so I stuffed it under my chair. Why do people want to live here?

Camilla, our teacher, arrived. She, too, had to unravel her scarf and peel off layers of clothes before we could start class. The other students were talking, mostly in Spanish, to each other.

"English!" she said loudly, but with a smile. "In this room, we speak English, remember?"

Everyone laughed. I looked around and began to appreciate my classmates and their desire to learn a language even if I would probably never need it. I studied English at the NPH school, but I remembered only a little of what I had learned. Our classes focused on grammar and a few English phrases, and as soon as we left the classroom, it was back to Spanish. Here, Camilla expected us to be able to write, speak and understand English. My classmates had chosen to live in the U.S. and would need these skills to survive.

Camilla was in the front, talking about strange phrases of English; words with two meanings like "right," one being the direction and the one that meant something you deserved. Or date, a day on the calendar but also a night out with a girl. Or leaves, things that fall off a tree but also when someone exits. It went on and on with words like "blue" and "type" and "fly." No wonder these people were hard to understand. English was stupid.

"Sam, tell me something about El Salvador in English," Camilla said. I think she called on me because she saw that for once I was looking up and paying attention.

I stared straight at her and felt everyone looking at me. I looked down like I was concentrating and then looked up, "It is hot and sometimes it rains."

"That's a great start," she said. "Next time, I would like you to tell the class three things about your country in English. Okay?"

"Yes, OK."

The class continued with Camilla going around the room, quizzing other people on words and sentences. Finally, it was over, and I grabbed my things and starting putting on Mel's coat. Camilla asked me to stop at her desk as I was leaving.

"Sam, I know from your tests that you are doing well understanding the written word. But you need to practice your English speaking by talking to others in class as well as your English-speaking friends when you're not here. That's the only way you're going to improve."

"Yes."

"I look forward to hearing the report on your country," she said, turning back to her work.

"How was class today?" Marlene asked when Mel dropped me back at the house.

"Good," I replied. "Camilla, our teacher, asked me to give a report on El Salvador in English."

"That's fantastic," she replied. "Will you tell them about NPH?"

"Yes, maybe."

Marlene was in a good mood as she made dinner. "Juan came through his surgery really well," she said. "His mouth has healed, and they were able to revise his lip. He will look really different next time you see him."

"That's good," I smiled back at her. I was happy that he was doing well. Soon I would be able to stay home in El Salvador for good.

"Tomorrow, after your classes, Mel and Mary Jo will take you to see him," she said.

"Okay," I replied.

Maggie was sitting at the kitchen counter, looking up at me

like she was thinking. She was the one person who always made me smile. It was the way her face twisted up when she had something on her mind.

"Sam, what does '*brazo*' mean?" she asked.

I rubbed my hand up and down and replied, "arm."

As I pulled up a chair, she laughed and said, "Sounds more like mom's bra to me."

I was afraid to laugh. "Let me see your work."

She was studying the names of body parts in Spanish and I started to quiz her. We worked our way down from the head and were going over the different parts of the leg. I could see she was losing her patience and realized she was having the same kind of frustration learning a new language as I was.

Ojo, Maggie, ojo," I said and laughed.

"What is *ojo*?" she said as she looked at the paper.

I pointed to my eye and laughed as I explained, "It is eye but sometimes it mean focus."

"Why do words have to mean two things in Spanish?" she asked in frustration.

"In Spanish? English worse," I said.

"What do you mean? Spanish is worse," she challenged.

"Really? How about your words, like "red" and "read" or "blue" and "blew?" Can be color and different meaning, like "I read a book, or "The wind blew." It was then I noticed I had the same problems in English that she had with Spanish.

"Yes, but everyone knows those words," she said.

"No, not everyone. You only know because you speak English since you were baby," I replied. I began to better understand that for everyone, learning a new language comes with challenges.

At dinner, I continued to quiz Maggie about the body parts. I saw Marlene smile at Brian as we went back and forth. She was getting frustrated, and I was laughing as we spoke in Spanish. Then it was my turn to be frustrated as we spoke in English.

The next morning, I was in the car staring out the window. It had snowed, and the snow was sticking to the tree branches and hanging on the bushes. We drove past a cemetery, and the iron fence around the property had a little pile of snow across the top beam. It was exactly the same height along the whole fence, like someone measured it and carefully placed it there.

Mary Jo was talking in the front seat; about the weather, the snow, Juan, a dinner party at their house and inviting Father Ron. I snapped back into the conversation when I heard he was coming. "When is party?" I asked. I wanted to see Father Ron and make sure he was still my friend. Since January, we had spoken to each other only a few times. I thought if I showed him I was trying, he would be happy. I hated feeling like he was out of my life.

I was still thinking about the snow when we entered Juan's room. He was lying in the hospital bed, watching television. They had repositioned his jaw, and he couldn't talk. It would be weeks before he could.

I walked in and felt a deep sense of guilt. For so long, I had been jealous of all the attention he was getting for his music and the concert.

I don't know if it was how bad he looked or the fact that he couldn't talk, but I walked over and put my hand on his shoulder. "Are you OK?" I asked him, and for the first time, I really meant it.

#

&

CHAPTER TWENTY-EIGHT

FATHER RON
CALLED HOME

A concert? I couldn't do it. I couldn't ask anything more from the team at NPH, especially since I was about to announce I was leaving El Salvador.

Sitting in my car in front of the Byrne house, I was trying to process what I had just heard. I realized I needed to drive away or Brian and Marlene might come out, thinking something was wrong. But I just sat there, recapping the last couple of hours visiting Juan.

I thought we had turned the corner with Juan. He had agreed to return, he was finally learning how to walk on his new legs, he had recorded the NPH song with Nick and we were almost finished with his surgeries. I felt like the whole project was coming together and wrapping up at the same time my stay at NPH was coming to a close. I was so happy to have seen it all through to the end.

Then, Marlene threw me a curveball. Actually, two curveballs.

I was already feeling tremendous guilt, like I was abandoning everything in El Salvador. Leaving the country. Leaving all the children. Leaving a mission I loved so much. How could I request anything more from these people?

When I arrived at the house earlier in the evening, Juan was looking swollen and bruised. The surgery on his face had been rough.

He was, however, in good spirits.

Taking a seat next to him on the L-shaped couch, I could see the recovery process was in full swing. "How are you?" I asked, staring into his eyes. On the table, there were medicines, water, Vaseline, another chart noting dosages and timing, with check marks in every column, ice packs and bloody gauze pads piled in a bowl.

From the look of the room, I assumed Juan would be crabby, but instead he seemed quite energetic. He was sitting up and holding his guitar. Next to him was his green notebook.

"A little sore here," he said as he touched his lips.

"It's only been a few days," I replied.

"He's doing really well," Marlene said as she entered the room. "The doctors told us the swelling and bruising are normal, and his whole mouth is in the best shape yet."

"I'm happy you are feeling good enough to play your music," I said.

"I must practice more for Nick," he replied, strumming the guitar.

"Is this for the NPH song?" I asked. "I thought you finished it?"

"No, for my songs," he replied.

Marlene jumped in. "Father Ron, Nick and Juan have been working together on his music. Nick wants to record the songs Juan has written and then produce a CD." Her excitement was evident. (Curveball Number 1.)

"A what?"

"A CD," she said.

"Can he do that?" I asked.

"Yes."

"Really? Isn't that expensive?"

"Well, it is. But Nick has asked some of his colleagues to donate their time. He has a studio, and he asked me to get some donations to help fund production of the CD."

"Can you do that?" I was surprised that Marlene would take on something more, especially given her schedule.

"I'm trying," she replied. "But there's more."

"More?"

Marlene looked over her shoulder at Brian, who had joined us. "Yes. Nick wants to have a concert with Juan to introduce the CD. The concert would be a fundraiser for NPH." (Curveball Number 2.)

So, that's the evening in a nutshell, which led me to be sitting in the car in the Byrnes' driveway two hours later, replaying the entire conversation, contemplating my next move. Somehow, Marlene had gotten me to agree to talk with Olegario about the concert. I would have to ask if Juan could make another visit just to perform. It would include an extended stay to practice with the band. This time it would be more than an uncomfortable conversation with Olegario and the rest of the group at NPH, it would be downright scary.

♪

CHAPTER TWENTY-NINE

SAMUEL
GREEN IS A BAD COLOR

The weather was perfect the night we arrived at NPH, and the place felt almost new to me. After spending 10 days in the cold weather of Chicago, I was enjoying the soft breeze on my face. It felt warm, unlike the evil winds of winter in the U.S. The more time I spent there, the less I liked the cold. It was fun at first, different. Now it was cold, and it hurt.

I was in the courtyard, talking to Olegario and Juan when I saw Eva. Her big smile said it all. Once I could escape the conversation, I walked over to her, still carrying my suitcase. We stood and talked about things that had happened since we'd last been together. Even though there was nothing really important, I hung on her every word.

It was the end of February and the arrival of spring felt promising as we would both finish our mandatory service year and then head to college in Santa Ana. I would be living in the boys' house, but we would be close enough to see each other during the day. The thought of going to college with her made everything so much more exciting.

I put my things away and was walking to the cafeteria, breathing the fresh air and catching the smells of dinner. Tomorrow,

I would be back to my regular routine, breakfast duties, then seeing to things that Father Ron might need. Olegario had already told me he needed some packages taken to Santa Ana. That would mean I'd get to drive.

The hustle of dinner with the clinking of trays mixed with the children talking and laughing made me smile. Compared to the quiet dinners with the Byrnes, this was so much fun. Here, I never had to speak a word and could feel like I was in a conversation. And the best part was I didn't have to speak English.

I sat down at a long table with some of the boys. They asked about Chicago. Their wonder about snow was endless. I found it very hard to describe. Every one of them wanted the chance to live in Chicago. Some had gone on the fiesta and bragged about their trip. The rest just stared as they listened to others talk about the cities, the families and the events. Boris was curious to compare what I did while I was at the Byrne's house, and he especially wanted stories about Murphy.

"I have to go to English school," I said.

"Who do you go with?" he asked.

"No one. Juan is usually at the hospital." I noticed Eva enter with the girls and sit down at the table across from us. They were chatting and giggling, but she looked over at me and smiled.

"But are other kids in the class?" Boris asked.

"Yes. Not just kids, though. Some are adults trying to learn English because they have moved to Chicago."

"Any girls?" he asked.

"No," I replied. It was then that I realized that I never really paid any attention to the others in my English class in Chicago. Because I didn't care about learning English, I really didn't care about the other people in class either.

Juan walked into the hall and came over to our table. I assumed he was coming in to eat, but he stopped right behind me.

"Did you see my green notebook?" he asked.

"Where? On the plane?" I asked.

"No, in your luggage," he said loudly.

"No," I answered without turning around.

"I need that notebook," he demanded, his voice raised.

"I don't have it," I said.

"How do you know? Have you unpacked everything from your suitcase?"

"Yes," I said and continued to eat. I knew it would make him mad.

"It's like my passport. You are supposed to be responsible for managing our things," he said. He was accusing me of losing this too. "You don't watch to make sure these things don't get lost. It's your only job on our trips."

I stood up quickly and got right in his face. "I am not responsible for your stuff. You're the one who loses everything." I knew I would never hit him. He knew it, too. But I was right in his face, not taking his accusations.

Father Ron came out of nowhere. He was almost running over to us. We both stopped talking. I didn't sit down though. I just kept staring at Juan.

"What's wrong with the two of you?" he said, and I could tell he was mad.

"Sam has my green notebook. Or he lost it, but he doesn't want to admit it," Juan said.

"I don't have it," I replied.

"And I don't really care," Father Ron replied, taking a deep breath. "Here's what I do care about. I care about important things, like how we treat each other. So perhaps you could figure this out without shouting and disturbing everyone else."

He turned around quickly and then stopped and turned back to us.

"What happened to the two of you? How did you get so selfish? So jealous of each other? You have each been given a gift, something everyone in here would cherish. It should make you grateful, better, more understanding. Instead, you have used it as an excuse to be jealous and unkind." With everything he said, his voice got louder and louder.

And he wasn't finished. "Beyond your little world, there are people facing real problems. For example, the earthquake in Haiti. There are families who have been crushed. Did you know that right now, at our home outside Port-au-Prince, your NPH brothers and sisters are worried about food, their home and their lives?" He looked at me. "There are children your age without water." Then, he looked at Juan. "There are people having their limbs amputated because they were crushed in the rubble. And here you are acting like this."

Suddenly, the entire dining hall was silent. Father Ron never yelled at anyone in public, and everyone was shocked. Then, he pointed to the door. We both knew what that meant, so we started walking with our heads down. I felt ashamed. I'm not sure what Juan felt. I had heard about the earthquake in Haiti, but I hadn't really thought much about it.

When we got outside, he turned to us. "I'm sorry I yelled at you in there. But you have both been blessed. Juan, there are people working so hard to help you overcome your physical challenges, not to mention making your music come to life. And Sam, the Byrnes have welcomed you into their home and their family. They've even sent you to school to learn English. Everything they are doing is for you, for both of you, and I don't see either of you appreciating what you have been given. In fact, you're both being mean, jealous and selfish. So, figure it out. Find a way to act like brothers."

He left us standing there.

"I will look for it," was all I said to Juan before I went back in to finish eating.

He nodded and headed off in the other direction.

I was greeted with the boys' teasing growls as I sat back down. I was ashamed they thought it was funny, so I didn't react.

When I looked over at Eva, she was staring at her food.

After dinner, I walked up to her and a group of girls. The weather was so nice I was hoping she would take a walk with me.

When we were alone, she turned to me with anger on her face. "You have changed."

"Changed? How?" I asked.

"When we first met, you were mild and kind. You cared about others. You didn't yell at people. Why are you different now?" she asked.

"Oh that," I replied, looking back at the dining hall. "I just didn't like Juan accusing me of something."

"You may think he sounded like he was accusing, but really, he just asked you about that notebook," she said, and I could hear the anger in her voice. "You are the one that started that argument."

"I'm always having to answer to him," I explained. "I don't think you understand what it's like traveling with him."

"I don't think you understand," she stated. "You were chosen to accompany him because of the type of person you are, or were. The Sam I knew wouldn't act like this."

"I didn't mean to upset you." I was apologizing, but she didn't seem to care.

"It's not just me you upset. Everyone in that room would jump at the opportunity you've been given. You throw it in all of our faces when you talk it down."

She started to walk away, and I held her arm, "What should I do?"

"You should stop being so selfish. Respect this opportunity. You should try to be nice to Juan, no matter what." She turned to face me. "I told you I don't give my heart away easily. I want to give it to someone who is kind."

"I promise right here, right now, I will try to be better with Juan and kinder to everyone," I said.

"Make something of yourself Sam rather than want what someone else has," she whispered. She grabbed my hand and we walked back to her dorm without saying another word.

#

CHAPTER THIRTY

SAMUEL
IT'S A TAKE

"That's not right," Nick wasn't yelling, but he was mad. Christina stopped and looked at him.

"What's wrong with it?" she yelled back at him.

"You're off the beat. Just listen," he said. Then he played back the song on guitar.

"That's what I did," she argued.

"No, it's not," Nick said. "This has to be right! Now, listen again!"

I think Juan liked it when Christina and Nick argued. At first, I thought it was because when they fought, Nick wasn't yelling at him. But I think he liked it when Christina stood up to Nick. Juan never yelled at Nick anymore. His attitude had changed, and they were getting along.

Christina threw down her drumsticks, stood up and ripped off her sweatshirt, threw it on the floor and then sat down again. "Fine! Let's go again," she yelled.

I loved watching her play the drums. I had never seen anything like it. The NPH music troupe had drums, but each drummer played just one drum. Christina sat with a whole set of drums and cymbals. They made her look small, but when she played, she moved so fast you could hardly see which one she was hitting.

They started to play again, and within a few seconds, Nick yelled, "That's it! You got it!"

Maggie had let me borrow her Nintendo D.S. so I would have something to do at the studio while the band practiced, but for the last 10 minutes, I had been watching Nick, Christina and Juan work. They finished recording the final song, and everyone was celebrating. I was celebrating the end of these long nights in the studio. I didn't always come along, but sometimes I felt I should just in case Juan needed me. After my argument with Juan and my talk outside the NPH dining hall with Eva, I was trying to be nicer. When we came back to Chicago, I starting helping more, and trying to have a better attitude about Juan. He was having some trouble with his new legs, so I decided to do some extra things, like helping him with his guitar case and delivering his clothes to the laundry room.

Nick went to the little refrigerator beside the couch and pulled out a bottle.

"Come on Sam, you're celebrating too," he said as he walked back into the studio.

I packed the Nintendo in my backpack, right next to Juan's green notebook. He had found it in the zipper pocket of his suitcase. I smiled about that, thinking how he must have felt discovering it was his mistake after accusing me.

I walked into the studio as Nick ripped the shiny paper off the bottle and started pushing out the cork. I ducked behind a speaker.

"Sam, you scared of a little cork?" Nick laughed.

"I think it will spray," I said, remembering the times I'd seen people open bottles like that in movies.

"Only if you shake it. And we want to drink it!" he said as the cork popped. Nick poured some into plastic cups.

The musicians were putting their equipment away, and Juan was sitting on a stool in the middle of the room. Nick handed him a glass.

"Well, Juan you did it," he said, touching his glass to Juan's. "It's a big deal finishing 10 songs and recording the tracks. How do you feel?"

Juan was smiling. It was the happiest I had ever seen him.

"Good, very good," he replied.

"There's still one really big job for you," Nick said. Juan looked puzzled.

"What do we call it?" Nick asked. "The album needs a great name."

"I don't know," Juan replied.

"Well, you have talked about doing the concert for Haiti. I think concentrating on the people from the earthquake, and those who lost limbs, is a fantastic idea. Does that inspire any ideas?" Nick asked.

I didn't know until then that Juan wanted to dedicate his concert to those in Haiti like him, amputees who had lost their limbs in the earthquake. I looked at him differently. Maybe Eva was right when she said he was not a bad person. Was I the selfish one?

Juan thought about it for a moment, then shook his head.

"What about you, Sam? Do you have any ideas?" he asked as he handed me a cup of champagne. It was sweet and bubbly, making my nose tingle.

"No," I answered. I had never tasted champagne, so I was concentrating on that. There was nothing I could say because this was Juan's thing, not mine.

"How about NPH? Does that give you any inspiration? You both talk about Father Wasson," Nick said as he passed out champagne to the other musicians as they sat in a circle around Juan.

"Tell the guys about NPH," Christina suggested. Juan smiled as she talked. He loved her.

Juan told the story about Father Wasson and how he started NPH by saving a young boy who had stolen the collection money from his church in Mexico. "The boy was the first *pequeño* at NPH," he said.

"We are all grateful for Father Wasson," I said after Juan told the story.

I had to admit, I loved the idea of giving Father Wasson credit for some of this. He had saved us all.

For the next 20 minutes, Nick and the band came up with names for the album. I sat quietly, sipping on my champagne, deciding I liked it. After I finished my cup, Nick poured me another.

Some of the ideas were crazy. But it was fun to listen to them.

"*Central Music.*"

"*Standing Up For NPH.*"

"How about the *Sound in the Central*?"

"*Music Has Legs*?" Everyone laughed at that one, even Juan.

"Well, we do need a name," Nick finally said. "Go home and think about it."

"What about *Gratitude*?" Juan asked.

"What about it?" Nick replied.

"Maybe we say thank you?" Juan asked.

Around the room, everyone was nodding. Nick looked surprised. "That's a great theme," Nick said. I could see he was really happy. It was the first time I realized Nick and Juan had become friends.

"The Sound of Gratitude," Christina said, almost to herself.

One of the band members repeated it in Spanish, "*Sonido de la Gratitud.*"

The room was silent, and then, Juan smiled and started to strum his guitar. He nodded and repeated it in Spanish. That was it... *Sonido de la Gratitud.*

Suddenly, everyone was laughing, even me. And then, I saw it for the first time since I had met Juan. I saw real gratitude in his eyes, as he stood up and hugged Nick.

"*Gracias,* Nick," he said.

#

♪

CHAPTER THIRTY-ONE

MARLENE
SAY CHEESE

Juan was delighted sitting for the photographer. We had purchased a crisp, white shirt, and it made his dark skin glow. I stood behind the photographer on the pavement in front of an old manufacturing plant as Juan positioned himself on a wooden bench sitting against the brick. We had scouted this location a week earlier and determined it would be an ideal backdrop for Juan's photoshoot.

I watched the photographer set up and wondered what this building once housed. I imagined the workers using the bench to smoke cigarettes during breaks, or maybe to eat lunch somewhere away from their work space.

I was sure it had never been part of a photoshoot. It seemed ironic that this orphan from El Salvador was using it to take a photo for a CD cover and a concert.

I looked closely at Juan. He had rolled his sleeves up to show off his strong arms. He was wearing a necklace, one I'd never seen. I wondered where that had come from. His hair was thick and perfect. We had gone to the barber for a cut, and he lathered on the gel to make it lay perfectly in place. His new jeans were accessorized by a brown belt that matched his new shoes. Without knowing about his legs, you might not even realize he wore prosthetics.

He appeared confident. And yet, when he looked at me, and especially when he smiled, I noticed something different about him. He was more vulnerable, more open. He seemed genuinely grateful.

Still, I worried that Juan had a Hollywood vision of this experience. With all the attention, I wondered if he thought he was about to be the new Ricky Martin or Enrique Iglesias. Were we doing the right thing by giving him this opportunity and all this attention? Was it too much?

I had tried to explain Steve Agueri to Juan. I played some of the Journey songs and told him he was the guy who replaced the band's original lead singer, Steve Perry. He had never heard of any of them, neither the guys nor the band. Then, I tried to explain Gina Glocksen to him. I showed him American Idol and told him how Gina was a finalist. Juan had never seen the show.

Nick had a lot of music connections, and after he explained Juan's story to them, these amazing artists agreed to perform at the concert. Nick wanted an event with great music, including Juan's songs. He knew a larger audience would be drawn to a group of artists performing rather than just Juan, an unknown. He planned to have some of the performers open the event, and then he would introduce Juan's story before Juan took the stage for his first American performance.

To us, Journey was legacy music, reminding us of our younger years, with lots of songs we could all sing along to. American Idol was a Hollywood hit, and truly one of the hottest shows on TV. But to Juan, this was all brand new. It was strange. On one hand, I worried that Juan's expectations might be too high, but on the other, I hoped he wasn't taking all this for granted.

As Juan perched on the bench, he pointed to his crutches, and I understood he was asking me to get them out of the shot. The photographer stopped me. "We need those next to him," she said. "It's a critical part of the story." As an advertising professional, I understood the value of visual storytelling, so I nodded and leaned them on the bench before I moved back to my position behind the action. Juan strummed his guitar, and as she started snapping photos, she was having him look down and then at the camera. He was delighted with the attention and the ability to "play the role of himself," a phrase I picked up from a friend.

Then, Juan held up his hand. He had an idea. He started to stand, grabbing one crutch and using the guitar on the other side. I was stunned at the brilliance of the idea, the combination of the crutch on one side and the guitar on the other really said it all.

The photographer was shooting everything, moving quickly, talking to Juan, changing lenses, getting the most out of the time we had. They were in a rhythm, and I knew without even seeing these photos that they would be awesome.

I realized, in that moment, Juan knew how to get attention. I guess he had done it all his life. A kid with no legs. An orphan. Born with a cleft palate. How did he get here? Become a musician? Write songs? His story drew people in, not with sympathy, but with respect and hope.

Over the past few months, so many people had contributed to make this opportunity possible. But in that moment, I realized Juan had grown to understand how to take advantage of these gifts in the best possible way. Perhaps it was his biggest accomplishment, learning to seize opportunity and use it to help himself. Father Wasson often wrote about preparing the kids with a foundation they could take into their adult lives. Juan's life would always include his disability, but despite his challenges, he had found a way to achieve more than most.

"Is that what this whole journey is about?" I thought as I watched Juan and the photographer work together like they'd been doing this for years. In some ways, this success was his and his alone. I would never again let anyone tell me how much "we" or "others" had done for him. This was his accomplishment.

A few weeks before the concert, things were too good to be true. Tickets were selling. The finished CDs had arrived and would be for sale to attendees. Only one thing had me concerned; Juan was extremely quiet.

So many people were supporting the event. The NPH staff and donors, Shriners Hospital employees, the Romero Center employees, UIC staff and others, not to mention our friends and family. Even the classmates from Sam's English class were coming to hear him sing. What if he couldn't do it?

"How do you even know he can perform on stage?" I asked Nick. "He has never had an audience like this before, where he was the featured performer. What if he freezes?"

"That's where I'm hoping his attitude—and frankly, his ego—kicks in," Nick said. "He may need that when he gets on stage. But I have created a concert that includes other artists. Even if Juan isn't great or can't perform, we'll still give them a show they can enjoy."

"But won't they be disappointed if he doesn't sing?" I asked.

"I have no doubt he will sing," Nick said. "He's a born musician. It's in his blood."

"I'm just not sure he realizes what an audience this size will feel like," I argued. "Nick, he's a kid who lives in an orphanage. Are we expecting too much?"

"I love it that you worry," he replied. "But let's make a deal: you worry about his recovery and rehab—and the ticket sales—and let me take care of the music."

I didn't see it. In my head, I couldn't envision the whole thing, the concert, the audience, and all these professionals coming together to support a guy with no experience. Then again, I didn't have a better plan, so I let it go. The idea that we would have these artists on stage with Juan, who could completely fall apart, didn't seem to faze Nick in the least. I would be a nervous wreck until May, I was sure of it.

It was going to be a long couple of months.

♪

CHAPTER THIRTY-TWO

SAMUEL
FRONT PAGE HOME STRETCH

I was heading upstairs with an ironed shirt on a hanger. Marlene told us we both needed to look nice for the reporter who was coming to the house. I didn't know why I needed to look good. They were coming for Juan, not me. I put on the shirt and noticed Juan was in the bathroom adding even more gel to his hair than usual.

He came out of the bathroom with his legs on and was rolling up the sleeves of his pressed shirt. "I wonder what they will ask me?" he said, as though I might have information about the interview.

I didn't say anything. I knew he loved all the attention, and I wasn't going to add to his ego. I also wasn't going to say anything mean. I had promised Eva I would be kind, and sometimes, being kind comes in the form of silence.

The reporter brought a photographer with him. I decided to sit in the dining room and watch from the table. Juan was on the couch across from the reporter, who was asking him about his music, the experience of recording his songs and the upcoming concert. In between, Marlene would answer questions about the surgeries and NPH.

As they talked, the photographer moved around the room, taking pictures. They asked Juan to sing a song, and he quickly lifted his guitar and started to sing.

I had to admit, he was a performer, and even though I hadn't ever told him, I liked his songs. It was a week before the concert, and the excitement was building. I knew the event would be good for NPH, so I tried hard to stay positive and support everyone, including Juan.

At one point, the reporter turned around and looked at me. "Sam, could I ask you a few questions?"

I got up and went into the living room. Juan stood up and walked out of the room, so I sat in his seat.

"Tell me about how you came to NPH," he said.

I looked at Marlene who nodded. "I was 10," I started. "I lived with a family after they found me in the trash. The man died and I was taken to NPH."

"You were in the…the *trash*?" he asked.

"Yes, I was born with a stomach infection, and my mother threw me away," I said.

He was stunned. "And who was this family?"

"The man, Jorge, found me in the dump as a baby. He brought me home, and I lived with them."

"That's an incredible story," he said.

I didn't say anything. For me it was just facts.

"How did the man die?" he continued.

"We delivered bread. Some thieves stopped us one day, stole Jorge's money and shot both of us." I pointed to the back of my head and showed him the scar.

As he looked at my head, Juan entered the room. This time, he was without his legs. He had gone upstairs to take them off.

I looked at the reporter. He immediately turned to look at Juan. It was always shocking the first time anyone saw him without his legs. The reporter immediately looked back at his photographer.

"Juan, is it okay if we take some shots of you without your prosthetics?" he asked.

"Yes," Juan said.

"How about if we have you play music?" he asked.

Juan pointed to his guitar, which was leaning against the couch, so I handed it to him.

I went to our room, took off the pressed shirt and threw it in the corner. Then, I realized it was my jealousy kicking in again. I picked up the shirt, flattened it on the bed with my hands to get out the wrinkles and hung it in the closet.

After the reporter left, Juan came into the bedroom. I was lying in my bed on the floor. I didn't say anything as he hopped up on his bed and turned out the light.

"I hope I can perform," he almost whispered. "I am scared."

All I said was, "I know." I should have said more but I didn't. He was nervous, and I knew he would never tell anyone else. As I laid there in a dark, I started thinking. "What if he can't perform? Should I tell Marlene? Or Father Ron?"

The whole night, I felt bad. I kept tossing and turning and thinking. I realized just how jealous I was of Juan.

Right then, I decided to stop. I would give up trying to compete. I was lucky. Eva and Father Ron had reminded me of all the good things in my life. I had my legs. I wasn't the one enduring surgery. I could hear Eva saying, "Make something of yourself rather than want what someone else has." I needed to be happy for him. More importantly, I needed to be happy for myself.

For the next week, Juan was quiet. I noticed he would take his guitar with him everywhere but didn't actually play. He went to practices but said nothing when he came home. I saw him reading his green notebook. I wondered if he was forgetting the words to his songs and needed to remind himself. His words kept going through my head: "I hope I can perform. I am scared."

On the Thursday before the concert, he came to bed very late. He had been at his final practice with Nick, and after, they were going to the theater to stand on the stage where the concert would be held.

I waited for Juan to turn on the lights. But tonight, he walked straight into the bathroom and shut the door. He was in there a long time. I listened but didn't hear anything.

When the door opened, I could see his shadow. He had taken

off his legs and was hopping up on his bed in the dark. I waited for a minute.

"Juan?"

"Yes?"

I took a deep breath. "I know you are scared. This is big," I started. He didn't say anything. "Just remember, you are really a good musician. Your songs are great, people love you, and the musicians are good. I have watched you this whole time, and I know you can do this."

He was silent.

"When you see them, the audience, just pretend you are back at NPH playing for the kids, the ones you sing to every Saturday night at Mass and at Christmas. Then it won't be scary." The room was quiet, and then Juan spoke.

"Thank you," he said quietly. "Sam, you are a good friend."

I lay their quietly, waiting to fall asleep, happy about Juan's words. Then, he spoke again.

"Sam," he said quietly. "I am sorry about Eva. I tried to get her attention to make you mad. That was wrong. I know you like her, and I know she likes you, too."

That night, we both fell asleep feeling better about ourselves and each other.

§

CHAPTER THIRTY-THREE

MARLENE
WHAT DOES GRATITUDE SOUND LIKE?

I came out onto the porch and saw Juan in two places at once. The "real" Juan was out there, supposedly practicing walking on his new legs. And, as I looked down to the morning paper on the porch, there he was, his picture on the front page of *The Chicago Tribune*. I couldn't believe it. I sat down and immediately read the article, and after, I couldn't stop looking at the photos. It was perfect. It painted a real and accurate picture of Juan's story, a story that would touch anyone.

Then I looked up, where the "imperfect" story of Juan was playing out. He wasn't practicing with his new legs at all. Rather, he was sitting down the sidewalk on a chair.

"Come on Juan, you need to practice."

If I didn't sit out here with him, he wouldn't practice, and even when I did accompany him, I had to constantly remind him to keep going.

Reluctantly, he stood up with his crutches. It looked strange because unlike his old legs, his new ones bent at the knees, and his gate was much different. Interestingly, underneath his pants, they looked almost real. They also made him taller. He loved that. But he didn't love this, the rehab and the nagging.

He started walking down the sidewalk. The goal was to replace the swinging motion of his hips that moved his old prosthetics to a kicking motion that would propel each new leg forward. It wasn't natural for him. He had swung his straight legs for years. The frustration was obvious.

"That looks good," I said as he walked toward me. It was the longest flat surface we had, and I had promised his doctor that I would have him practice an hour a day. I also promised we would make him wear the new legs as much as possible. That was the hard part. Juan liked to go back to his old legs when he felt lazy, which was often. The new legs required him to think—and practice—constantly.

Juan passed me on the sidewalk as though I wasn't there. I had set up chairs at both ends of the sidewalk in front of our house. He walked back and forth and sat down when he needed a rest. Most days, he "needed" to rest more than he walked. It was a never-ending battle between two stubborn people.

"Keep going. You've only gone three times," I yelled as he ended his pass. If I didn't keep track, who would? It was like coaching someone who hated the sport he'd signed up for.

Juan walked back and forth a few times and then stopped in front of me.

"You read the story?" he asked.

"Yes. I can't stop reading it," I smiled. "It's amazing you are on the front page of the paper."

"How many coming to concert?" he asked.

I had also been reviewing some of the concert materials while I sat outside. This project had taken over at work. The staff was really excited about helping; in fact, everyone was. But I still had an agency to run, and it was occupying much of everyone's billable hours.

"I don't have a count on tickets, but we're getting a lot of calls and requests." He was peering over my notes. "Are you nervous about the event?" I asked.

"No." He smiled. "I'm so happy with the music now. I am glad you asked Nick for another chance." He turned and continued down the sidewalk.

For the next 20 minutes, he walked back and forth. When he was walking toward me, I kept my head down. When I could look, I watched him struggle with each step. The legs were heavy, or at least they seemed heavy to me. So many questions crossed my mind when I looked at him. Why did he have to lose both legs? Why was his amputation so high? It complicated everything. Does he remember the pain of being burned so badly? How does God give so much to some people and so little to others?

I was reading the rest of the newspaper when Juan finally walked over and sat on the porch steps.

"Do you know about the earthquake in Haiti?" he asked. "There was a terrible one."

"Yes, I read about it, and I've been keeping up on what's been going on there since," I answered.

"NPH has a home there," he continued. "And a hospital for children."

"Yes. They have been caring for both children and adults affected by the disaster," I said. I knew about Haiti, NPH and St. Damien's Hospital. Information about the work being done there by staff had been sent to all the sponsors involved in the NPH organization.

"Did you know they have had to amputate many limbs for people?" he asked.

"No, I didn't know that," I replied.

"They have limbs crushed in the rubble. Just like mine were in the fire."

I had never talked to Juan about his legs.

"Do you remember the fire?" I asked. I knew Juan was very young when his house caught on fire, and his legs were burned.

"Some. I remember being in hospital. I remember pain."

"Were you there a long time?" I assumed he would have been a patient for an extended time.

"Yes. They good to me."

The door had been opened for me to learn more. "When did you get your first set of legs?" I asked.

"At NPH."

I knew he had not come to NPH until he was almost 12 years old. It meant he didn't have any way to move around before then.

"How did you walk as a child?" I asked.

"I had a *patineta*," he said as he moved his hands along his sides. "I don't know English."

It took me a minute to understand, "A skateboard?"

He nodded. "*Sí*. A skateboard."

"That was smart," I said, picturing little Juan pushing himself around.

"I have a question," he said, "but I don't know if I should ask."

"It's okay. You can ask me anything," I answered.

"Who gets the money from the concert?"

"Well, we agreed the money from the CD would be yours, and the money we make from the concert would go to NPH, right?"

I wanted this to be Juan's decision. It was his concert, his music, and his choice, but I also felt I couldn't let him change his mind now. We were too far into this, and what's more, we'd announced it to the world.

"I just want some to go to NPH in Haiti to buy legs and arms for those children; the ones who lost them in the earthquake," he said.

I took a deep breath, needing a moment. "Juan, that is beautiful," I replied and reached out to touch his knee. Of course, I realized he couldn't feel anything there, so I grabbed his hand. "I think we can make that happen. I will talk to Father Ron."

Juan smiled as he started into the house. Then, he stopped.

"Can I talk to Father Ron about it?" he asked.

"Yes, you can. It will make him so happy," I said.

At that moment, I decided that no matter what it took, I was going to make this happen.

At breakfast Sunday morning, I was trying to listen to Maggie talk about her art project, but I couldn't help looking out the window every couple of minutes. I was waiting for Juan to return. He and Sam had gone to Mass with Father Ron, and I knew Juan was going to talk to him about the donation to Haiti.

Finally, they returned. Before they were even fully in the house, I blurted out, "How was Father Ron?"

"Good," Sam replied. "He go back for another Mass and said say 'hello' to you." I waved from the doorway as Father Ron drove away.

Next, Juan entered and sat next to Maggie. "So?" I asked.

"He said he ask Olegario about donation," Juan replied. It was nice to see him smiling as well. "But he very happy."

A week later, Father Ron called me. "So, was this donation to Haiti your idea?"

"No. This time, it was all Juan," I answered.

"Progress. That's what that is," he replied. "I have been trying to get Juan—and Sam for that matter—to think about someone other than himself. I guess I'm making an impression."

"You sure are. Can I tell him it's approved?"

"Yes, you can. In fact, I think you should use it as inspiration for his performance. He's nervous."

When I told Juan that Father Ron had called to say they could send money to Haiti, it made him very happy. He reiterated the whole story of asking Father Ron, and I could tell he was proud of himself, but not in a cocky way. Brian could see it too, and winked at me from above his newspaper.

It's those moments, the tiny ones where you feel a connection, when you're happy or you make someone else happy, that kept me going through all of this. With Juan, I realized how much I had hung onto these moments throughout the three-plus years he had been coming to stay with us.

Juan was now a "regular" at our parish, singing at Mass with our choir. Today, before we entered, he told me he was singing a song in English, and I should listen carefully.

At communion, Juan started playing the guitar. This was it, *Make Me a Channel of Your Peace*, a beautiful hymn. As he sang and played, I realized I had never really listened to the words this closely.

I couldn't take my eyes off him. It was beautiful. Juan looked up and stared straight at me, singing one passage directly to me: *In giving to all men that we receive.*

It spoke to our situation, to Juan's change of heart and to everything that NPH represents.

It was what Juan had come to understand about this journey; all the wonderful gifts came together around Juan and Sam during their time with us. What was so clear to others reading the *Tribune* story had become blurred to me.

Now, as the experience was coming to an end, all the fatigue and arguments were forgotten. What remained was what we had achieved. In that simple sentence, I came to understand the incredible gift I had received.

#

CHAPTER THIRTY-FOUR

FATHER RON
STAGED BLESSING

The Park West is an old Chicago theater. As I walked up to the front door, I thought about how many musicians had played here, famous and unknown, in all music genres. And now, it was Juan's turn, and I wasn't sure what to expect. Before that moment, I hadn't really realized the unbelievable turn that his life—and his story—had taken. But here I was, arriving at what would be his first live public performance, a kid who years before had little chance, if any, at a productive life.

In my head, I could envision the crowd cheering and dancing. I hoped there would be enough people to make it feel full of energy, but I wasn't sure. How many would come to see an unknown boy who didn't even speak the language, singing songs no one knew?

I wanted to see Juan before he performed to give him encouragement, be a friendly face. As I turned the corner from the parking lot, I noticed a news truck on the street. Then another and another. Could they be here for him? For us?

The ticket booth was staffed with young volunteers, and I recognized a few faces from the NPH Chicago fundraising office. They had helped Marlene and her staff promote and organize the event. The proceeds would be divided between NPH and St. Damien's Hospital in Haiti, just as Juan asked.

"Hello, I'm Father Ron," I said to the young woman situated just inside the entrance.

"Oh, yes," she replied skittishly, as though I'd caught her off guard. Immediately, she turned and yelled over her shoulder, "Father Ron is here!"

"Father Ron, I'm Danielle, it's so nice to finally meet you," she said as she shook my hand. "I'll escort you to Marlene. She wants to introduce you to a few people, but she might be hard to find."

"Hard to find?" I asked.

"Yes, we're expecting over 500 people tonight," she replied.

I stopped in my tracks. "500?"

"Yes. And right now, Marlene, Juan and Nick are all busy with the media," she continued as she led me up the inclined walkway into the theater.

She pushed aside a set of black curtains and I followed her through. There were throngs of people milling about in the seats and at the two bars set up in the back corners of the theater. Stagehands were moving equipment with a full house of guests waiting eagerly in the lobby.

"This way," she said, grabbing my elbow. "*The Chicago Tribune* story about Juan has generated a lot of excitement."

Across the lobby, news crews were getting into position. I spotted Marlene doing an on-camera interview. I saw Juan not 20 feet away from Marlene, talking to what appeared to be a newspaper or magazine reporter.

Marlene finished, and Danielle moved in to catch her attention. When she saw me, her expression went from business-like and focused, to happy and relieved.

"Can you believe this?" she said. "I'm overwhelmed, excited, scared and worried all at the same time."

"It's amazing," I replied even though my feelings were exactly the same as hers. We both knew Juan. Could he really pull this off? And if he didn't, what would happen?

Marlene turned to look at Juan. "I hope he can do this. Do you think he can?"

"Yes," I said as flatly and confidently as I could. Priests have a way of being positive in tough situations. My theory has been to stay positive with the fewest words possible. Otherwise, you invite doubt into the conversation.

"What if he doesn't? What should I do? Should I go up on stage and apologize?" I couldn't tell if Marlene was talking to Danielle, me or to herself. "Nick says they have a few extra songs to play in case, but it won't be enough to cover the whole length of the concert." She looked panicked.

"They seem to be having a great time already," I said.

Marlene was whisked away to talk with someone else. I stood watching Juan, trying to get into his head. Was he ready? Would he freeze on stage? Did he have any idea how many people would be here? Or what that would look like—feel like—when he was on stage? The only time I'd seen him perform in front of a group was with the NPH music troupe, and there, he wasn't the star. Did he understand how different this would be?

As I watched him talk to the reporter, he was smiling and laughing. A young woman was sitting next to him, interpreting to make sure each understood the other. He didn't look nervous on the outside, but Juan was known for not showing his emotions.

A tap on my shoulder revealed a group of donors who had visited NPH in El Salvador. Mel and Mary Jo were with them, reintroducing me. We spent time talking about the event and Mary Jo telling us about the discovery of Juan's talents at the hospital. When I turned around, Juan was gone.

I walked through the foyer and back into the theater, where I spotted Sammy. When he caught my eye, he fought his way through a tangle of people and nearly tackled me. After hugs and a quick discussion about the event, I looked around for Juan and asked if he knew where he had gone. "I want to talk with him before the concert."

"Maybe back there?" Sam pointed to the stage. "I show you."

As we made our way down the aisle and toward the stage, I was stopped multiple times by concertgoers who recognized me. Sammy waited patiently at each stop, much like he used to wait on me in El Salvador. I realized just how many people Juan had touched on his quick trips to Chicago: members of the Byrnes' parish, friends of their family, the doctors and nurses at Shriners and UIC, and NPH donors and staff. So many had been affected by his story.

As we went backstage, I pulled a curtain to the side to take a look at the setup. The drum set was larger than I expected. There were stands and mics, guitars and a piano. It looked like something for a bigtime rock band, not a kid from an orphanage. The weight of it made my stomach turn, and now I realized exactly how Marlene felt. I panicked a bit for Juan.

"He is back here," Sam said.

There was Juan, leaning against the wall with his crutches looped around his forearms. He seemed quiet and hadn't seen us yet. I nodded to Sammy, who understood he should leave. He backed away, and I started toward Juan.

"*Hola*, Juan."

Juan looked up at me and smiled. I could see him let out a sigh.

"*Padre*," he said, holding out his hand. I shook it and pulled him in for a hug.

"I am proud of you, Juan. You have done something very special, for NPH and the people in Haiti," I said.

"Thank you. I am happy to do it," he said. These were words—and an attitude—that I hadn't heard from Juan. I was impressed, and proud.

"Are you ready?" I didn't want to use words like "nervous" or "scared," so I thought "ready" was my best option. It was best not to put anything remotely limiting or negative into his head.

"Yes, I think so," he replied.

"Will you pray with me?" I asked, putting my hand on his shoulder and squeezing.

"Can I talk first?" he asked.

I nodded.

"I know you do this for me. The surgery. The families. Every-thing," he said, looking me in the eyes. "You are the one who make it happen, and I have not been very kind. I want to thank you from my heart. The music I play, I play it for you and NPH."

"Juan, that is beautiful," I said, doing everything I could not to get too emotional. "Just like your request to help the amputees in Haiti, these things are the meaning of gratitude like we talked about on the bus all those years ago."

He smiled, and then, we bowed our heads.

Dear God,
Be with Juan and all the performers on stage tonight.
Fill their hearts with confidence and send their message of love.
Bless all who have given of their time and treasures to make this concert happen.
Those who are attending, and those who are performing,
And all the staff behind the scenes.
It is only together, with each other and with you Lord,
That we make wonderful things happen.
Amen.

After the prayer, I shook Juan's hand, and he pulled me in for a hug. "*Padre*," he asked, "would you do something for me?"

"Anything, Juan."

"Would you hold this for me while I play tonight? I want to make sure it safe."

I smiled and accepted the notebook, his prized possession, the home to all of his original words and music. Then, I watched him as he turned to embark on the biggest night of his young life.

I looked down at the notebook, staring at the green cover. It reminded of my prized childhood possession, that green bike that had been taken from me all those years ago. Suddenly, with that tattered notebook in my hands, my disdain for the color green faded. I held it to my chest and went to take my seat, protecting it with my life.

#

♪

CHAPTER THIRTY-FIVE

MARLENE
CURTAIN CALL

"**W**here's Juan?" I was panicked. No, I was freaking out. The days leading up to this event had been more than chaotic. Juan was quiet to say the least. Maybe angry. Maybe scared. I wasn't sure. Nick was juggling musicians, equipment and rehearsals. We were all on edge.

I should have been happy with all the attention. Tickets had sold. Friends and family were here. Groups, like the staff of Shriners and the El Salvadoran Consulate, had stepped up in a big way. Musicians had volunteered their time. Nick had been so right about Juan's story. Once we started to tell it, it was like a snowball. The media picked up on it. The story in *The Chicago Tribune* had driven interest. People wanted to see the stars who had volunteered, but they also wanted to know more about Juan. They wanted to see him perform.

Once the story hit the newspaper, television stations came out of the woodwork. There were trucks from every major network affiliate, including the Spanish stations, lined up on the street in front of the Park West Theater.

I walked to the front of the theater near the stage as people entered. Danielle, Nick's wife, was there and I asked her if she had seen Juan. She shook her head and continued to greet people.

I kept my smile on, hugging everyone I knew, thanking them

for attending. I kept looking over their shoulders for any sign of Juan. Where had he gone?

I headed for the stage. I was afraid to ask Nick, but I was desperate. We had to get Juan backstage soon. He seemed nervous all week, and I thought he would need a moment to collect himself.

I went to the green room. It was bustling with energy. Steve Agueri had arrived, and everyone was excited to meet him. Christina introduced me, and I thanked him for making this event bigger than we ever imagined. I was so nervous it didn't hit me until later that I actually hugged the man who had been the lead singer of Journey.

I continued down the hallway to find Juan. I went backstage where Nick was examining the setup.

"How's it going?" I asked with a put-on smile. He was sweating and still in his "work" clothes, putting the final touches on the stage.

"We're almost set," he said. I could tell he was stressed out.

"Have you seen Juan?" I asked as nonchalantly as I could.

"Nope, not back here," he replied as he moved a piece of gear.

I walked across the stage, deciding to make a circle back to the front from the other side of the theater. As I walked down the stairs, I noticed a small room off to the side. I peeked around the corner and there was Juan. He was standing with Father Ron, who had his hand on Juan's shoulder. Both their heads were bowed, and it was obvious they were praying together.

I couldn't hear what Father Ron was saying, but the scene was so peaceful. It was the first feeling of peace I had all week. I stood and watched in silence. I could feel myself relax. In that moment, for the first time, I felt like this could all be OK.

When they finished, Juan looked up at me. We both smiled. I nodded.

"There are some more reporters who want to speak with us," I said.

For the next 30 minutes, Juan and I talked to reporters, repeating the story about his past, the surgeries at Shriners and the music. During the interviews, I could see friends and colleagues entering the theater. Juan still seemed nervous. He kept looking around, searching for someone. I was a wreck.

"We need to get backstage," I told him as I waved to people in the crowd.

"I need to find Sam," Juan said.

"I think he's here somewhere, but I don't know where." I looked around.

"I have to find him before I go on," he demanded.

Just then, Matt walked by. I told him to find Sam and bring him backstage to me.

Juan and I made our way to the front of the theater, eventually arriving on stage, behind the curtain which separated us from the audience and the chaos. At that moment, we were both emotional wrecks, but we were in it together. In reality, I had never felt closer to him. It felt like the end of a great journey.

Nick left to change clothes, so we knew we had a little time before the start of the show. Then, Juan grabbed my hand. "Thank you, thank you for everything," he said. I reached out and we held each other for a long time.

"Are you okay? Ready?" I asked, wiping my eyes and plastering on the biggest smile I could muster.

"I need Sam," he said. This time, he was almost begging.

I peeked through the curtains, as if I would be able to find him. The seats were filling up, so many faces I recognized. The doctors and nurses from Shriners were in the front row. The NPH staff from the Chicago office were off to the left. Our friends, neighbors and people from our parish were also getting seated. I saw the teachers from the Romero Center, even the Consulate General from El Salvador.

"I don't know, Juan," I said, and then, from the side of back stage, Matt and Sam appeared.

Juan turned his body to face Sam.

"Thank you. I am glad you are here with me, not just tonight but for the whole time," Juan said. "I don't think I would be here without you."

"You can do this," Sam said, smiling. "I know you can do this.

I know you will do this. Just keep saying that over and over. It works. Say 'I can do this', OK?"

Juan nodded and smiled, that same genuine, grateful smile I first saw at his photo shoot. The boys shook hands. Then, Sam put his hand on Juan's shoulder and pulled him into an embrace.

Nick appeared on the other side of the stage. It was time.

Juan started walking.

"No Juan. You are supposed to enter from here," I whispered, "after I introduce you." It didn't matter. He just kept walking.

When he reached Nick, he put both hands on Nick's shoulders. I could see them talking, and Nick was smiling.

Behind the curtain, Nick handed me the microphone. I would start the event with a thank you. I had written and rewritten it for weeks. How do you thank all these people? Who should I list first? How do you convey the importance of everyone in this moment? The doctors were here. Father Ron was here. The musicians. Nick. There was no way to let everyone know just how grateful we were. I had always been able to speak in public. I had been a reader in church when I was young. I had presented to clients. I had given speeches for NPH. But tonight, I was tongue-tied. I think it's easier speaking to an audience of strangers. But these were people who knew me, they knew Juan, they knew our story. I could never do it justice.

I listened to the banter on the other side of the curtain. Everyone was talking, and the energy level was rising. I nodded to the stage manager that I was ready. The house lights dimmed, and the crowd started to get quiet. Then, the curtains opened just a crack, enough for me to step forward into the single spotlight illuminating center stage. Luckily, with the light shining on me, it was difficult to see any single face in the crowd.

"Thank you all for being here tonight. This journey—Juan's journey—is what brings us all together. But what tonight represents is much larger than that. There are more than 3,300 children in the nine NPH homes, being cared for like Juan, being cared for by an organization that is changing the world. Tonight, we celebrate their work and see how it changes lives. Juan's music would never have been heard if not for so many people. Father Don, who introduced him to the surgeons at Shriners. The surgeons who fought for a grant to fix his cleft palate for free. The Mulliganeers who donated the funds for Juan to travel back and forth. The nurses who cared for him. Father Ron, who orchestrated the entire effort from El Salvador. And that's just the medical part of this story. Then there's the intern at Shriners who gave Juan his guitar. There's Nick, who brought Juan's music to life. What started as scribbles in a green spiral notebook are now songs on an album. And tonight, a concert. Juan's story does that. It inspires everyone to be better. It inspired the incredible artists to be here with us tonight for the latest leg of this journey. And speaking of "journey," we are thrilled to have Steve Agueri, who was former lead singer for Journey, perform for us, as well as American Idol's Gina Glocksen and Chris Medina. They are all donating their talents to sing with Juan tonight.

Before I leave this stage, I want you all to help me thank Nick Vitogiannes. His talents go far beyond the music. He brings it all together with his vision, leadership and drive, that's why we are all here. I hope you enjoy the music tonight. But more than that, I hope you carry the deeper message out into the world much like Juan does. When you get the opportunity to say 'yes' like all those involved tonight, I hope you do. Thank you, and welcome to *The Sound of Gratitude*."

I thought once I finished my speech, I would relax.

The show started with a video about Haiti and NPH. It told the story of NPH and their homes in nine countries. It explained the tremendous tragedy in Haiti after the earthquake. How the hospital was caring for victims. How amputations, much like Juan's, were a major part of keeping people who had been trapped in the rubble alive. Juan was on screen explaining how he wanted proceeds to go to their efforts and help others like him, amputees, innocents whose lives were changed due to tragedies they could not anticipate or control. He wanted them to receive prosthetics to walk again.

I watched as the audience took it all in. They were somber.

Nick had said the band would play a "warmup" song to start

the night and get the audience seated. He wanted to bring them back to the fun of the evening before introducing Juan. I think I was even more nervous because as the curtains opened and Nick started the first song, I was still unsure Juan could perform. I had no idea what would come next.

From the side of the stage, I watched it unfold, feeling lucky to be near the back door, like I could use it as a quick escape.

The music started. The band performed without Juan. Just as Nick had planned, the audience was getting fired up before Juan even took the stage. Nick knew the value of building suspense, excitement and expectation, and with each passing moment, that's exactly what was happening. "Juan doesn't have that many songs, so we need to craft a concert that both introduces him and entertains," he had explained to me weeks prior.

I could see Juan waiting in the wings across the stage. Waiting. That wasn't always a good thing. From here, I couldn't tell how he was feeling.

"And now, I give you Juan Manuel Pineda. The man of the hour!" Nick introduced Juan as though he was a top-tier rock star. A member of the crew put a stool down center stage as Juan walked out on his crutches with his new legs.

He sat down to a standing ovation. He didn't smile. As he put the guitar strap around his shoulder, he looked at Nick. I took a deep breath and held it. It was Juan's job to start, and he just sat there, looking down at the guitar strings. The audience was quiet, holding its collective breath.

I don't think I will ever again in my life see something like what happened next. It was magic. Juan's fingers started flowing over the guitar, softly at first as the band chimed in. He was sitting up tall. His voice was perfect. He smiled, a beautiful smile given to him by Shriners and UIC. He was as happy as I had ever seen him. A performer. A *man*.

The audience was riveted.

The song ended, and again, Juan sat still, stoically looking down at his guitar. The musicians were waiting for his signal to start the second song. But this time, they appeared much more confident following his lead.

He leaned into the microphone. "I want to say *gracias* to all of you. It not always easy, this surgery, this music," he said, looking back at Nick. "But I love you all more than you will ever know." Then he strummed the guitar and the music started again.

I never really understood the concept of performing live, and the energy it gives entertainers. I can't play anything but the radio. But I felt something that night. I stood backstage for the first half of the concert and just took it all in. Christina on the drums, completely in her own world. Nick playing the guitar with so much passion. Juan with his head bouncing to the music.

Eventually, I walked around the theater and stood up in the empty balcony by myself, for the first time seeing it from the audience's view. They were having a blast. Juan and the other performers had the crowd on its feet, clapping, dancing and singing along. Steve Augeri had the place up for grabs. Everyone was singing. Once again, Nick's concept of blending songs with Juan's music was perfect.

And in a blink of an eye, it was over. But it wasn't just the concert. All of it was over. His face was fixed. He was standing on new legs. The CD was published. His last song was sung, and there he stood, leaning on one crutch. He was beaming.

And then, it happened. Alone and safe in the balcony of that beautiful theater I felt it. It was the warm release of tears, all the tears—from all those years—coming out as I watched Juan raise his arm up in victory...and gratitude. The crowd was going wild.

It was finished.

EPILOGUE 2020

JUAN MANUEL PINEDA

Juan Manuel Pineda performed "The Step Forward" concert on May 13, 2011 at the Park West Theater in Chicago to raise funds for Haitian amputee children and adults, and NPH. It is estimated that between 2,000 and 4,000 children and adults endured amputations in Haiti as a result of the 7.0-magnitude earthquake on January 12, 2010.

Volunteer performers included, Steve Augeri, Journey lead singer from 1998-2006 and successful solo artist; Chris Medina, Season 10 American Idol contestant; and Gina Glocksen, the 9th place finalist on Season Six of American Idol.

Juan donated his profits from the concert to NPH and to St. Damien Children's Hospital and the pequeños in Haiti. The hospital had performed countless amputations, managed rehabilitation efforts and provided prosthetics for those injured in the devastating earthquake.

Juan returned to El Salvador in 2011 with the profits from his CD and lived at NPH for another year. When he left, he became a music teacher and taught English. He was married on Christmas Day in 2016. He continues to promote his songs and perform, working as a music teacher in a small village in El Salvador.

SAMUEL JIMENEZ COREAS

Samuel became proficient in English during his time in the U.S. In fact, Camilla, his teacher, recommended advanced schooling, and the Byrne family offered him the opportunity to attend college in Chicago. Eva helped convince him to study abroad.

Sam came to Chicago in late 2011 to study at the DePaul English Language Academy. In passing his TOEFL college entrance exam, he was accepted at Northeastern Illinois University, where he earned his bachelor's degree in social work.

Because of the relationship with Patricia Maza-Pittsford, the El Salvador Consulate General in Chicago, he was offered a position in the diplomatic offices in the El Salvador Consulate in Chicago and accepted a five-year assignment to work with immigrants of El Salvador residing in the United States. Sam lived with the Byrne family until the summer of 2020, when he got married.

BISHOP RON HICKS

Bishop Ronald Hicks became involved with NPH following his college graduation when he volunteered at NPH Mexico for one year. After being ordained a priest, he served in the Archdiocese of Chicago. In 2005, he began serving as Regional Director of NPH in Central America and he accompanied the NPH music troupe to Chicago for a fiesta tour. He returned to Chicago to work in the Archdiocese of Chicago where he began his career.

On September 17, 2018, Father Hicks was ordained a Bishop by Cardinal Blasé J. Cupich and became the Vicar General of the Archdiocese of Chicago. His coat of arms includes a representation of his time at NPH and the children he lived with and proudly served at the NPH homes in El Salvador and the surrounding countries. He is now Bishop of the Diocese of Joliet, Illinois.

Bishop Ron continues to support NPH and visits the homes regularly.

MARLENE BYRNE & FAMILY

The Byrne family helped Samuel enter DePaul and Northeastern Illinois University. He lived with them until the summer of 2020 when he was married. He continues to work for the El Salvador Consulate. Matt and Maggie graduated high school and went onto to college.

NPH

NPH operates residential care homes for vulnerable children in Bolivia, Dominican Republic, El Salvador, Guatemala, Haiti, Honduras, Mexico, Nicaragua and Peru. Since 1954, NPH has raised more than 20,000 children, changing their lives and helping them become leaders in their own countries.

In a changing world climate, countries have looked to NPH to increase services and reach out to communities with programs and services for those in need. NPH expanded educational opportunities for non-resident children, providing healthcare resources and countless other services to more than 170,000 children and families living in poverty.

Thanks to the financial support of its loyal donor base, NPH continues to reach the underprivileged in Latin America and the Caribbean. Driven by the core principles of founder Father William Wasson, NPH has established a reputation for quality care and created a culture of family both inside and outside the homes.

Support for NPH means an opportunity to break the cycle of poverty. It means raising leaders in their own communities who will affect change far into the future. It means NPH can offer community services to reach those in desperate need.

How to Donate:
NPH USA
134 North La Salle Street
Suite 500
Chicago, IL 60602-1036

www.nphusa.org
1-888-201-8880

MUSIC HAS LEGS

We hope you have enjoyed the story of Juan Manuel Pineda.
He and so many of the pequeños of NPH inspire us all to reach for
better lives.

We hope you will share this story by recommending the book
to your friends, family and colleagues.

www.musichaslegs.com

Watch for our next book on
www.goodstoriespublishing.com

ABOUT THE AUTHORS

DAVID HAZNAW

David is a full-time writer and author, amateur musician and sports fan. He loves the craft of storytelling, and his style takes you into the mind of the character. Over the past 25 years, he has written and produced video content and corporate communications projects for clients across the U.S. As part of this story, David wrote and directed a video about Juan's life journey and his premier music performance in Chicago.

In 2019, David published a book of creative nonfiction titled, *A Year in Words* crafted from his commitment to write an essay every day for an entire year.

David and his wife, Joan, have two adult children (Kate and Will).

MARLENE BYRNE

Marlene has been writing her entire life for both fun and work. She published five children's books about backyard games under the Project Play umbrella. She has also written books for clients, and recently released a book titled, *Change the World. Start with the Children.*, about Father William Wasson, the priest who founded Nuestros Pequeños Hermanos homes for orphaned and vulnerable children.

Professionally, Marlene is the CEO of Celtic Chicago, a full-service branding and marketing agency. She has balanced motherhood, career and service throughout her life. Her charity work led her to the Board of Directors for NPH USA, where she would accept the opportunity to care for Juan Manuel Pineda.

Marlene and her husband Brian have three adult children (Samuel, Matthew and Maggie) and a dog named Riley.

Marlene Byrne and David Haznaw met 25 years ago, working in advertising. Both writers by trade, they worked on crafting headlines and stories for clients.

After years of writing for others, the two decided to become partners and worked to craft the story of Juan's journey in *Music Has Legs*. They are currently working on a book about Sam. Juan's story has touched so many lives, they hope it will touch yours as well.

Made in the USA
Middletown, DE
16 September 2021